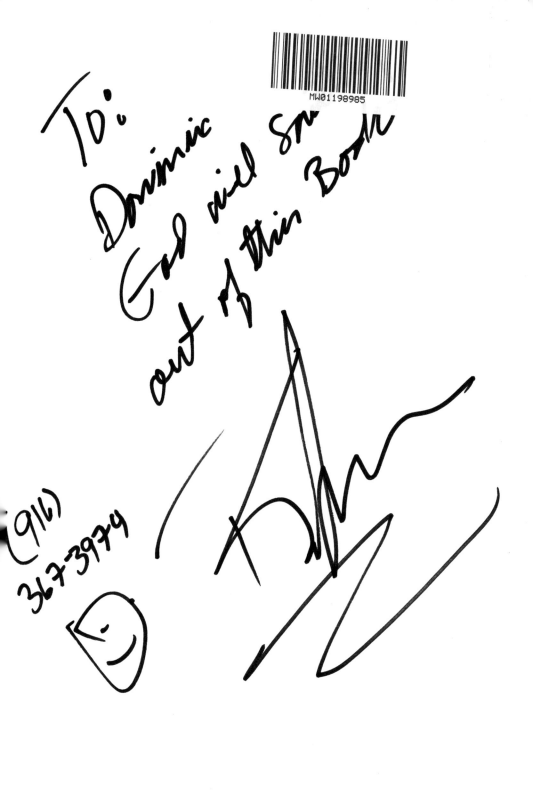

To:
Dominic
God will Sm...
out of this Book

(916)
367-3979

RALPH SANDERS

outskirtspress

DENVER, COLORADO

To Lauren Sanders,
my loving wife and mother of my beautiful daughter.

You always amaze me with your wisdom when it comes to our family. Your career achievements are a blessing. I am proud of your hard work. You have demonstrated the willingness to go beyond yourself and offer support and attention to my dreams and success. Not to mention, you encourage me not to give up daily, which I thank you for. You are very loved!

To Greg Scott, a dear friend and boss, you offered me a job over all others. Thank you for your support and commitment to see me through financially.

To Richard Wells, my high-school coach, the man who taught me the rudimentary skills of basketball. I appreciate your discipline in coaching, which helped me to receive full scholarship offers in the past.

I want to give special mention to Joe King, a Christian "brother" and dear friend, who gave me the privilege of keeping hope alive at a time of darkness and silence in my life.

I want to acknowledge my family. Although I don't see you all as much as I would like, I love you all. I would like to thank Pastor Ray of Bayside Church for

your great enthusiasm and your preaching—it brings joy and laughter to the saints of Christ.

Also Pastor Sherwood of Boss Church of South Sacramento, who is an anointed man, your preaching brings conviction to my heart.

Last but not least, Pastor Cole of Capital Christian Church of Sacramento, who will always hold a special place in my heart. You were there when I needed counseling in my new walk of faith.

You are all brilliant, God-loving people, and I am so thankful to have your wisdom in my walk. God Bless.

Acknowledgment

I am very grateful for all those over the years who were so dear to me during my challenges, struggles, and fears. You all have helped me see the future so bright. I thank God for all of you. My memories are full of respect and continuing love for my mother, Donna—may she rest in peace. I miss you, Mother, and your unconditional love; your love and enthusiastic spirit have made me the man I am today. I will always love you.

My heart is filled with admiration and thankfulness for the powerful defense provided by Michael Wise, Timothy Woodall, John Brennan, and Ron Ask, all attorneys-at-law, who did a great job proving the facts of my case. Without all of you with your expertise and your caring, I would not be experiencing my freedom and potential today. Thanks for your brilliance! I am overwhelmed.

Introduction

Have you ever met a person who appeared to be something that he wasn't? Someone you trusted, someone you liked, and someone you looked up to? Only to learn later that you had been deceived? I was that person. A *"Half-time Hustler."*

Honest on one hand and deceptive on the other half—real good and real bad at the same time. It was through this deception that I landed in prison.

In this book you will learn about a man who encountered one hindrance after another. He was blinded by how California's Three Strikes Law would affect his life. These obstacles and laws prevented him from reaching the goals he'd dreamed about since his teenage years, like getting into the NBA. Instead this naïve, unsuspecting young man ended up in a godforsaken place where he had to deal with so many disappointments and shattered dreams. I was that young man. If I'd only known back then to take my life more seriously and not be so deceptive, I would not be writing this book.

In my darkest moments of silence, I have seen others around me experience suffering because of low self-esteem, constant focus on the negative, and feelings of inferiority or inadequacy. These individuals always dwell on some reason why they can't make it instead of why they can. I have learned that no matter where you are or what challenges you face, you can truly enjoy your life! That is why I am writing this book.

Over the many years of losing my freedom, something made me grab hold of my future. There was a time when I was forced to make the best out of my situation, which was filled with adversities and trials. I knew that in order to expand my vision and survive, I needed something in my life that would guide me through setbacks and heartaches so my future would be much brighter than it appeared. God was that something!

I know today that there is a true purpose for facing all my trials. No matter how successful we are, we all face challenges and struggles. I started understanding that God had a divine plan for the obstacles that crossed my path. I believe he allowed me to go through them so I would know Him better.

Temptations and difficulties eventually come into everyone's life. However, with the right attitudes and motives, you can overcome the adversities of your environment. "For I know the plans I have for you, declares the Lord, plans to prosper you, and not to harm you, plans to give you hope and a future" (Jeremiah 29:11). It's through the storms of life that you will come to realize what your character is truly made of and how it connects to your choices.

Although my past was filled with setbacks, I have overcome these obstacles through right choices and faith in Jesus Christ, who I came to know while incarcerated. You will discover that I still face the Three

Strikes Law today. However, there are choices which we all must make in the challenges life presents to us.

In this book, I am sharing the truth of my past. The stories in it are real and from a real hard walk of faith. I have found myself in unknown territories, willing to follow God, through the biggest hindrances of my life. The Scripture says, "DON'T BE AMAZED AT THE FIERY ORDEAL THAT'S TAKING PLACE TO TEST YOUR QUALITY AS THOUGH SOMETHING STRANGE WAS HAPPENING" (1 Peter 4:12). I pray that God may bless the one who reads this.

Table of Contents

1

Looking Back

Sitting in a 5′ x 11′ cell in San Quentin State Prison, West Block Reception Center, I visualize writing a book about my life if I ever make it out of here. It will be God's calling for me to do so. There is so much I need to tell and share.

Thinking back on my childhood, I realize it wasn't very bright. Coming from a family of six brothers and one older sister was quite different from the families around us. It seemed to me that my mother was doing the best she could. I never understood why my father was never around, or why even my brothers' or sister's fathers were never there. What a story to talk about.

As the lights go off in my cell and I hear the correction officer yelling "lights out!" I can hear the echoes and whispers of everyone else around me in their cells. I am housed on the fifth tier in cell 423. My cell is at the end of the tier. It's a two-man cell and I have the whole cell to myself. Some of the inmates are singing out of boredom. When you are locked up in a cell, it's as if you are closed in a closet in your house, forever. The songs are really good as I lay back on my bed with my feet hanging over the edge of my bunk. My toes are starting to get cold from the breeze on the tier. The beds are really hard and made of steel. The mattress is three inches thick—so thick that even a dog would not want to lie on it. But it is something I have gotten accustomed to quickly. I have no choice since I have a five-year sentence to do. We are all wearing orange jumpsuits. My jumpsuit doesn't fit me too well because I am 6'7".

As I fall asleep I think to myself, I hope I won't be here when I wake up. I am numb to the feelings of what is really going on with me. Someone yells across the tier, "God is our refuge and strength, a very present help in trouble" (Psalm 46:1). This all feels like a dream, or a movie. Well, Good night.

As I remember my past in Riverside, California, Canyon Crest, I remember playing with my younger brother at the huge house on a circle. I was riding my bike. I can't remember which brother it was, but it was one of my younger ones. I also remember my older brother Lamont who used to eat dirt—or maybe I was the one… *Yes, it was actually myself!* I remember my brother Jamal rode his bicycle down the hill, fell off, and busted his chin; blood was gushin' out. He got in trouble from my mom for that—after going to the hospital to be stitched and patched up, of course. That's all I can recall in that house on the circle. I don't know for sure but I can't think that far back, but I think I was just five years old. (It was a long time ago.)

As time moves on, I remember living in Lennox, California, a Hispanic town located right next to LAX. I remember my oldest sister, Cynthia, doing laundry, and me and my little brothers running and playing around the house.

Cynthia is yelling at us, "Clean up and do your chores!" It is hard to remember much about my mother being in the house, but I clearly remember my sister. Boy, she surely took the place of my mother. I was about eight or nine years old at the time. I remember hearing planes from LAX constantly flying over the house. What a loud sound! My sister's boyfriend Tony (along with Cynthia) used to take us to football games at Lennox High School. I was too young to realize whether or not he was good for my sister, but they were together. My mom used to come home—although I don't remember if she had a car or not. I don't even know if she worked or not; however, I do remember she was always gone. She used to walk us down the street on the weekends to the discount clothing store called The Valley Village.

Boy, did they have an abundance of clothes! Everything from shoes to pants, suits to jackets, summer to winter; and all for really cheap prices. We would all hold hands when we crossed the street. We were like the Three Bears with Mama Bear. I remember Lennox Police Department across the street from the intersection we used to cross. It wasn't the best neighborhood to live in, but I assume it was affordable enough for my mother and my siblings.

As time went on, we moved to a three-bedroom apartment on 111th Street and Prairie in the city of Inglewood. At the time, I was about 10 years old. I recall that this was when things got really difficult for me. I was kind of teased a lot. There would be a yellow bus coming to pick me up for school. This bus was for Special Ed. students, and I was the only one on that bus. My brothers didn't have to take it. I can hear the horn going *beep-beep* and my sister rushing me out of the house to get on the bus. It's funny, because I remember I used to wear my favorite brown shirt, which I wore ALL the time. I would wear it inside out so I was nicknamed "Inside Brown" because my last name at the time was Brown.

One day in class, my older brother Gregory, who was a tutor in one of my classes, was upset about me being in the class (I never understood how he got in my class as a tutor). He complained to my mother about it. However, this didn't make a difference; I remained in the class because I was in Special Ed.

I used to love going to the Tropicana Bowling Alley off of Prairie. I recall stealing quarters out of my mother's purse to play Pac-Man at the arcade. Sometimes my mother would find out and put a stick to my ass (*Ouch!?!*). *We called it a switch!*

My mother had a boyfriend at the time named Castle. He was a big guy and looked like he had just paroled out of prison. He used to always fight with my mother and I'd thought he was crazy about her. He jumped through the sliding glass door one day because my mom had locked him out. My interpretation of this was that she wanted nothing to do with him any longer. I guess it was too hard for him to accept.

Betty was my mom's best friend. She was a woman who owned property next door. My mom would always run to her and talk to her for advice about Castle. I really didn't like her for some reason, but I don't know why. I guess I sensed some negativity around her in my consciousness—but it was all a blur. After that terrible time my mom locked him out, Castle seemed to have disappeared. I also remember my sister was kicked out of the house for fighting with my mother. She packed her bags and moved out with her Lennox High School football star boyfriend, Tony.

We had a dog, "Dandy," who was black and white. Boy, did we love him! But my mom didn't like him too much. He would make messes in my mom's living room and she would have a fit! No one messes in my mom's living room. It was like her paradise. We couldn't even sit in there. It was more like a showcase. Almost like having to go on a game show and win it! You may think I'm joking, but boy this was real.

One morning we woke up and Dandy had passed away on the back patio. Painful feelings developed in me, feelings that I never knew I had. My brothers and I loved Dandy. He was a great dog. We were kind of close with other people in the neighborhood, like "June-bug," Lisa, and their mother, Loretta. They were close friends of ours. Every neighborhood must come to an end. My mother moved us to Hawthorne, California, which is only 10 miles away from Lennox. That was a much better neighborhood. This was where my two little brothers and I attended Cimmaron Elementary School. I noticed real growth developing at age 10. I began understanding things at this time, such as street life. I assumed everything around me was truly how life was supposed to be. My environment wasn't a good example for me, and it definitely wasn't the truth. Still, my father wasn't around. What was I supposed to believe? Where was my father?

My mother decided to send us to Missouri because my father wanted my younger brother, Jamal, and I to live with him. My dad was in the Air Force and always in uniform. Going to Missouri was my first time on an airplane; I remember how high we were in the air and my brother and I were fighting over the window seat before the plane took off. I thought it was pretty cool that the ladies on the plane always smiled. It was one of those big planes with a second level. The flight was very long—I don't think I slept at all. I was too curious about this airplane and meeting my father. My brother Jamal didn't seem too inquisitive about anything. He just sat there in the window seat he stole from me, staring blankly out the window. I don't quite remember meeting my dad when we arrived there. It's almost as if my mind drew a blank too. With all the years of drama, headache, and pain, I find it difficult to remember certain details of my life. I think I mentally blocked out these painful memories in order to cope. This was a new experience for me. We watched television together, talked, and spent a lot of time with each other. My dad was a teacher on the base, and he would bring us to class. Jamal and I would sit at the back of the class reading a book in order to stay occupied.

At Christmastime, in 1977, I met my grandparents for the very first time. We flew to Washington, D.C., to see them. Thinking about it now, this was such a happy time in my life. I experienced family, home-cooked meals, playing in the snow, and opening presents on Christmas Day. I met cousins I never knew—my family seemed so large and close-knit.

While in Missouri, I attended fourth and fifth grade at Knob Noster Elementary. It was there that the teachers discovered I was dyslexic and had a learning disability. Here in Missouri, I was not in Special Ed.—the teachers worked with me. I presently got in touch with my dad, and he prepared this letter, which fills in a lot of information that I never knew about my childhood. After reading this letter, I was somewhat devastated at what I learned about my life. It brought tears to my eyes. My dad tried really hard.

RALPH IGNATIUS SANDERS
Illegitimate son born Feb. 4, 1968, in Riverside, CA, to:

- Ralph Ignatius Brown Jr. (hereafter RIBJR) (U.S. Air Force) and Donna Marie Crain.

- Given RIBJR's first and middle and last name of Carl Sanders, another man Donna was seeing when she met RIBJR. Her reason: she didn't want to hear RIBJR's mouth about Ralph's parentage after RIBJR and at least one friend of hers had questioned RIBJR's paternity.

- Third youngest child and one of seven children of Donna Crain (all but two were illegitimate).

- Survived a coma and a temperature of 105 degrees at the age of one with the possibility of brain damage.

- RIBJR moved into a single-family home to accommodate himself and Donna's growing family.

- Donna was manipulative and developed a closed-minded mindset she did not progress from. RIBJR offered to pay for schooling for Donna to acquire certificate and license for interior decorating because Donna was born with the God-given talent of an interior's eye. However, she never accepted the offer.

- RIBJR was reassigned to the Philippines in May 1970, when Ralph was two years old. Shortly after, Donna's youngest child was born.

- While in the Philippines, RIBJR and his three "sons" were nothing more to one another than voices on the phone, except for when their mother wanted money.

- From the Philippines, RIBJR was subsequently reassigned to New Mexico, Florida, Korea, and Missouri. Through all those assignments, the manipulative scheme of Ralph and his brothers asking for money long-distance continued; even though RIBJR was voluntarily paying child support at an amount higher than the law prescribed.

- Throughout this period, RIBJR attempted to have his children come stay with him during the summers. His efforts were always met with an emphatic "no."

- While assigned to Whiteman AFB, Missouri, a magical thing happened. RIBJR received a phone call from Donna, screaming at him to come get his kids (while calling him and her kids "every name in the book except the child of God"). RIBJR caught the first thing smoking to California and returned to Missouri with his oldest and youngest children (at the time), with the stipulation that it would only be for the summer. RIBJR had no intention of returning them to CA if I could help it.

- Thus he began a new life for my sons and I. Shortly thereafter,

RIBJR and his sons drove to DC to meet their East Coast family. They got a taste of what life outside the ghetto was like. If he remembers correctly, it was Christmastime. By then, he had enrolled them in school. As stated before, RIBJR had no intention of returning them to CA. Their mother was fuming and threatening him with legal action.

- Their first year in school had a rough start. When they were tested for academic achievement, it was then that Ralph was found to be dyslexic, which was something that was not dealt with in California because his mother was in denial. They also discovered that his brother had "adult female attachment" syndrome. As long as an adult female was standing near or providing him with attention, he could or would do anything asked of him. He was a very smart kid. By the end of the year they both began to improve immensely. Everybody loved Ralph. He was such a great kid, student, and helper. His aim was to please.

- When they first came to RIBJR, all they knew were the streets of Los Angeles. School in the ghetto was a joke. However, because of the excellent sufficiency of the Missouri education system (one of the best in the country) their progress academically improved greatly, almost overnight.

- During this same time, RIBJR taught Ralph the rudiments of basketball. He had some idea of the game, but no one had ever taken personal interest in his ability. Ralph thrived on what RIBJR taught him. He was a quick study. RIBJR coached his little league team, his first organized team experience. Allow me to make a point here:

We were having an intra-squad practice one day and the other team kept stealing the ball from Ralph. RIBJR could see he was in pain and beginning to get upset. RIBJR called a time-out and called Ralph aside for some personal coach time. He didn't like the way they kept stealing the ball. RIBJR asked if he knew why they were able to do that. Ralph had no idea. Ralph was the tallest kid on the team, if not in the entire league. RIBJR told him to hold the ball over his head and called the rest of the team back to practice and told them to get the ball to Ralph because no one could jump high enough to get the ball. RIBJR explained that the reason they could steal the ball was because Ralph was holding it too low. The rest is history. Ralph was already the leading rebounder in the league, and now no one got to steal the ball from him. It also allowed him to look around and locate someone to pass to, or shoot the ball himself.

- Alas, all good things must come to an end. RIBJR received orders for reassignment to Korea, he was to marry again, and his new prospective bride was not feeling the prospects of starting a family with an 11- and 9-year-old child. They were sent back to California to finish their childhoods. Though he tried, RIBJR was never able to get his children again for the summer.

- From Korea, RIBJR was reassigned to the Philippines again. During that tour of duty, he had occasion to be sent to the States (California) to attend a conference in San Francisco. He was bumped from a standby seat and forced to layover until a new flight could be identified. RIBJR took advantage of the situation to see his children. While in L.A., he and the boys made plans to hang out, play ball, and enjoy each other's company. However, Ralph's mother had other ideas. She refused to allow us to be together and asked RIBJR to leave. He did.

- From that point on, RIBJR never saw his children again. The phone calls looking for a handout continued, but he was not allowed to really talk to his children. He talked to Ralph a few times while in high school and college, but had no idea what Ralph was into at the time until he received a phone call from Ralph looking for assistance in the legal process. By then it was too late. After that, RIBJR believes they talked a few times while he was in prison. It is mind-numbing when your child is in a situation in which you can't help him out of.

- The next time RIBJR communicated with Ralph was some time after he was released. He told me of his marriage, sent some pictures; we conversed for a time and then another lull in our relationship. RIBJR tried reaching him, but by then phone numbers and e-mail had changed. Then Ralph called again, which brings us to this point. That's my story and I'm sticking to it.

Receiving this letter really cleared up some unanswered questions I had. However, it was hard to receive and I cried upon reading it. Having your whole frame of mind shifted from you by one letter can completely blow your mind, especially if you've been hurt by the thought of that person you thought intentionally left, to realize later that they actually loved you and wanted to be with you.

In the sixth grade I remember my history teacher, Mrs. Long. She was a heavyweight woman with an Afro. I remember I had a crush on Tamica Thomas at the same time; she was in my sixth-grade class. I think this was my very first crush. I also remember my younger brother Jamal in the fourth grade (his class was at the back of the school) and my older brother Gregory. Gregory brought Jamal home after talking to the principal about Jamal's behavior in class. I also remember my other brother Ray, who was in the fifth grade, was quiet. I saw him during recess and we would talk from time to time. As time passed, I finally went to a junior high school called Henry Clay. This school was on the other side of the railroad tracks called the Devil's Dips. Thinking back, it reminds me of the railroad tracks in the movie *Stand By Me*. Devil's Dips separated the golf course and "different" neighborhoods in Hawthorne. Sometimes I would travel by myself to school, and sometimes I would be with my brother Gary. I used to hate going by myself because I was afraid of the Crips, or other scary people who could steal from me. I used to wear my older brother's Fila jacket, gold chain, and gold watch. I didn't ask to wear them, but I would sneak and take it and wear it to school because I thought it was cool.

My classes were in the bungalows located in the front of the school. This is where the Special Ed. classes were. Believe me, math was one of my worst subjects. I just could not get it right. That was the same year my dad was coming around for Christmas and bought us Christmas gifts and spent a day or two at our house or at a hotel. That was the last time I saw my father for a very long time.

The longest house we lived in had three bedrooms; my older brother Gary, my two younger brothers Ray and Jamal, and myself all stayed there. I remember my mom getting a Cadillac Seville. It was so bright! It was yellow. It seemed that we were moving so quickly from house to house. But this was my mom's first house that she bought that I can recall. We lived there for a long time.

My mom was dating a man named PeeWee at that time. One day her and her boyfriend, PeeWee, came back from Vegas and had a lot of money. This PeeWee guy was loaded with cash. I saw him as an older man, but maybe 'cause I was so young. He always wore a hat—not a baseball hat, it was more like a bucket hat. He really liked my mom. He dished money out left and right. I mean hundred dollar bills. I think he even bought her a car. I was too young to know.

My brothers and I played baseball at Hollywood Park down the street. I was sorry in baseball; at least that's what everyone was telling me. I couldn't hit a ball because, for some reason, I was scared of fast little objects coming at me. My two younger brothers were good at baseball. We all played in the park league. I guess these were the things that kept us out of trouble and gangs in the neighborhood called the Crips. Our neighborhood was called Neighborhood Crips. My friend Todd, who lived right across the street from the park on my same street, was a friend of mine.

He came from a Christian family. His parents used to take him to church on Sundays. We hung around a lot and he became one of my best friends. Todd was a good kid who had a lot of potential in football. He was bussed out to an out-of-county school called Grant High.

How lucky he was because I had to stay in our city school district. His dad was an umpire of the baseball league at our park. Mr. Barr was his name. He was a good Christian man. I will never forget their huge dog named Misty. She was a mustard-colored Great Dane. We used to take the dog for a walk but Misty was so large, it seemed like she was walking us! I have fond memories of Todd and his family.

Around this same time, I began raising and collecting pigeons. I remember having a lot them, probably 30 or more. The guys in the Hood named me Big Bird because I had a long nose, I was really tall, and had a lot of birds. That was the thing back then—to have the best birds and watch them do tricks in the sky and come tumbling down. They were called "suiciders," and it was such a cool thing to watch by all of us kids in the neighborhood. I remember my mom did not want me having them any longer and I had to get rid of them because they made a huge mess, which I didn't clean up. I kind of lost interest in my birds after getting in high school and playing basketball, which was a new thing to do. Baseball and birds just don't work out at all. I was turning over a new leaf and becoming a teenager in high school. I began playing a lot of basketball on the court just about every day since we lived so close to the park. Basically, I started living and breathing basketball. My freshman and sophomore year in high school, I grew three inches—from 6'4" to 6'7". Wow! I started dunking the ball with no problem and tearing down the rims in the park. There were some good ballplayers in the hood; I learned from the best. To name a few, Elden Campbell, who played for the Lakers for five years; Jarvis Bassknight, who was the all-defensive player at UNLV; Gary Johnson; Harold Minor (Baby Jordan) from the Miami Heat; and Sean Higgins of the San Antonio Spurs. I always wanted to meet Magic Johnson. I used to love watching him play on television.

High school was fun and it was keeping me off the streets. It really was an adventure for me. I was never a good student; in fact, I mean, I flunked the eighth grade. When I started high school, I focused more on the social and athletic parts of school. I was active on both the track and basketball team, but basketball soon became my primary outlet. I spent much of my time practicing and playing basketball, which helped to make the varsity team as a freshman. I remember being picked up in a van by the assistant coach of the team. He would pick up several players like myself who lived in the hood and had no transportation to school. We were like a family. We were a strong team and won several championships. My best friend, Will, was also on the team and we spent a lot of time outside of the gym, partying and doing normal high-school things. We were referred to as the Twin Towers due to our being the tallest and best players on the team. Ironically, he lives only about 20 miles from me currently, and we still hang out at times and reminisce over the good old days. Unfortunately, during my senior year, I was forced to leave the team due to ineligibility. Because I was held back a year, this made me too old to play in my senior year. Coach Wells was devastated, as I was his strongest player. He arranged to send me to a junior college in Yuma, Arizona. They had a very strong team, and the intention was that I would play for them while I got my GED and then transfer to University of Arizona on scholarship. It was devastating for me to leave high school early.

Things didn't work out the way I planned that summer. I did not get my GED so I came back home and enrolled back into my high school. It was 1987 when I graduated. It was sad being there and only attending classes while my team played without me. High school was fun overall and I was highly respected, but my senior year was a challenge in that I felt lost and needed to find my place.

Many universities were still writing me and sending me scholarship offers to attend their schools, but I didn't have good enough grades. It's sad because UCLA was one of the schools I really wanted to go to. I didn't realize how disappointing it was when told I couldn't get in because of my low grade point average.

2

Collegiate Life

I remember the summer of 1987, a couple of months after I graduated, my brother Lamont packed up all my bags, put them in his
Camaro, and drove me all the way to Foothill Junior College in Los
Altos. It took a long time for me to get there—I think we got lost.
We finally made it to our destination and met the head coach, Eric
Vollmers. My brother had a connection with a close friend of his that
he grew up with in Riverside named Chris Harper. He was a good
basketball player at Oregon State University, a good Pac-10 college
called the Oregon Ducks. Actually, that was one of the colleges that
highly recruited me out of high school. My older brothers used to
take me to watch Chris play when Oregon State was playing USC in
Los Angeles. I was in high school at the time. I always looked up to
Chris even though I didn't know him that well. It was just because
we were both basketball players. For some reason, he got a job as an
assistant coach at Foothill Junior College because his career didn't
seem to go anywhere. Chris was my connection to Foothill. In my
freshman year, I was one of the best players in the conference. I received a lot of letters my freshman year from universities all around
the area such as Stanford, University of San Francisco, San Jose
State, and Cal Berkeley, just to name a few. It seems that I started

Travel, law and basketball

Sports profile:

By PAUL MAHEHOLZ

Ralph Sanders caught the coach's eye when he showed up in the 9th grade as a 6'5" freshman. He continues to catch the coach's eye as this 3'7" Foothill College star is averaging nine points, 11 rebounds, and two blocked shots a game. He has received offers from five schools already, including San Jose State, St. Mary's, and the University of Texas.

Sanders' stats reflect his love of defense, and he chose Foothill based on their 15-2 record last year. He loves the sport of basketball, but also enjoys the travel and fame.

"It gets me knows," he said. Sanders also sees basketball as a way to finance his college education.

Sanders also enjoys playing for new head coach Eric Vollmer and the new assistant head coach Steve Siler, formerly at Oregon State. Sanders also works after school in the gym, as a maintenance man.

Sanders would like to get into the NBA but isn't counting on it. He is enjoying school and working towards his major, Law and Society. He may try and play in the professional league overseas. During the off-season, Ralph runs track to keep in shape.

my new life, met new people, and adapted to a new environment, which was the opposite from where I grew up. I liked the trees on the campus and the people that surrounded me. Foothill had an awesome football field. There were huge and expensive homes all around the area. My freshman year was interesting because I was getting my stride and becoming a man on my own, adapting to different races, environment, and a much better life. At the time, this was the best place for me to be.

Foothill was a good fit for me. The structure of the program was exactly what I needed to keep me on track. I had an excellent counselor, Bobby Chavez, and every quarter he would go over my grades with me to ensure I was achieving at least a "C" average so I could continue to play basketball. My major was Law & Society, which my counselor helped me choose. I really enjoyed going to basketball practice, but I didn't get along very well with some of the players. I think there was a little jealousy due to the fact that I was a freshman and I was taking other people's positions that were sophomores.

During this time, I met this guy named Raj who was a senior at a local high school. He was playing tennis on the courts at Foothill. He admired my game and read about me in the paper. He stopped me on the way to the locker room and began talking to me about my game and where I might go to school. He invited me over to his house, which was like a mansion. It had a pool, spa, and basketball courts. We became really good friends and his family took me in as their own. I was welcomed in their home at any time even if they weren't there. They had really nice cars and nice things in their home. I really loved these things—it was a far cry from what I had growing up.

During my sophomore year I was devastated: I was let go from the basketball team by Coach Vollmer! My partial scholarship was lost! Around that same time I somewhat innocently began writing checks from my own account, not realizing there weren't enough funds to cover them. There weren't any major repercussions from this, other than having to pay back about $800 or $900. Fortunately, I was still able to complete my Associate of Arts degree in Law and Society so I was ready to transfer to a four-year university. I had many offers from excellent colleges, but chose San Jose State University to complete my undergraduate degree and play basketball. Around this time, I met a girl who attended Stanford University. I admired her because she came from a wealthy family and was on the crew team. She became my girlfriend and I got to know many of her friends at Stanford. We had a blast crashing parties and hanging out on campus. Stanford was so much better than my school. I loved it there! One day, I was in one of the dorm rooms at Stanford and I noticed a checkbook lying out in the open. I got the idea that I would take one of the checks from the back of the checkbook so it wouldn't be noticed. How was I going to cash this? Well, I had gone out partying in the city the night before with my ex-teammates from Foothill. We went out in my cool new Mustang that my brother Lamont helped me to purchase. The following day, I was cleaning my car and noticed my ex-teammate's ID in the backseat. I had this awesome idea (so I thought) that I would use it to pass the check. So I went ahead and wrote it for about $200.00 and headed over to the bank. My plan was to look for a young and pretty teller so that I could possibly distract her with my charm and good looks in order to cash the check without going through the normal requirements. It worked! I cashed the $200.00 check with no problem! Since I was able to do this without much difficulty and without getting into any trouble, I began stealing more checks. I never broke into anyone's room—I was always invited in. I probably wrote and passed about eight checks ranging from $200 to $300 each. I used the money to support myself.

Times Tribune staff photo by Craig Konfress

Foothill freshman Ralph Sanders goes up for a shot as Skyline's Jeff Anthony tries to block it from behind. Sanders had a game-high 12 rebounds in Foothill's 64-58 upset.

Ex-Foothill basketball star arrested on theft and forgery charges

By MICHAEL GARDINER

Former Foothill basketball player Ralph Sanders was arrested April 4 by Stanford University Police and charged with 16 felony counts in connection with recent thefts at Foothill and Stanford University.

Sanders, 22, faces eight counts of burglary, seven counts of forgery and one of false impersonation. Most of the cases involve Stanford students and all involve similar scenarios.

Stanford University Police Detective Tim Frecceri said, "the arrest was not the culmination of the case but instead really opened it up." Frecceri said he believes an investigation is underway at San Jose State University as well, where Sanders is currently enrolled. "I've talked to some other police departments in the Bay Area and in Los Angeles (where Sanders attended high school), and I think we're going to see a dramatic increase in the number of counts against him."

Although Frecceri says Sanders was arrested at Foothill in November after forging a check to pay a fine, he doesn't believe Foothill is conducting an active investigation of him. Foothill Campus Safety Manager Tom Conom was unavailable for comment.

According to Frecceri the case dates back to mid-late November when Stanford Police received reports of several dorm burglaries,

Ralph Sanders

and the victims all described the suspect as a very tall black man.

Frecceri said Sanders allegedly entered unlocked dorm rooms and casually began to talk to students,

(See SANDERS, page 12)

It didn't even occur to me that I should stop stealing blank checks from the dorms. It was as if something came over me and I had no control. I had everything in my hands—a great school and other schools that were extremely interested in me to attend their university and play basketball. I started practicing on the team as a walk-on at San Jose State and was making great things happen for myself; yet there I was, stealing from Stanford students at the same time. "**Halftime Hustlin'!**" My girlfriend and I decided to move in together off campus. We lived in a nice apartment a couple of miles from school in Palo Alto. We shared it with one of the girls who also went to Stanford.

My memories of this time are bittersweet. I was the "first" for my girlfriend in everything. We used to take walks and talk about the future. We planned what we would do after we graduated and how we might get married and things of that sort, you know—love stuff. I never met her parents because she was from back east, and she never met my

Sanders' bail raised to $150,000; hearing next week

By MICHAEL GARDINER

Ralph Sanders, the former Foothill basketball player arrested April 4 on theft and forgery charges, appeared in court in Palo Alto on Tuesday afternoon to enter a plea, and got an unexpected ruling from Judge Timothy Hanifan.

The public defender had asked for a superior court review of Sanders' case, telling the judge that his family was securing private counsel.

After looking over the documents of the case for a few moments, Hanifan said, "The bail in this case is too low... the bail in this case is way, way too low. I'm going to increase it to $150,000."

Sanders, whose bail had been dropped from $75,000 to $60,000 a week earlier, simply shook his head in disbelief at the decision. His brother, who had come to the arraignment from Los Angeles where the family lives, had a similar reaction.

The 6-foot-8-inch Sanders stood well taller than everyone in the courtroom as the judge granted the

(See SANDERS, page 12)

family either. I lied a lot about who my family was and told her I came from a wealthy background. In my mind, it was important for me to continue to impress her. This *Halftime Hustlin'* and lying was becoming a part of my character and I didn't feel guilty about it.

Going to basketball practice at San Jose State and attending school there was fantastic! A new arena was built and I was thrilled to play in it. I couldn't wait to play the U.N.L.V. basketball team! I was looking forward to making our team better with the season starting. I played some good games for the Spartans.

During the middle of the season, the students from Stanford began complaining about their wallets and checking accounts having less cash in them. I had no clue what was going on. Additionally, some of my teammates were asked questions by the officer on our campus one day. They never knew I was to blame, and honestly I really had no clue that the cops were investigating my thefts because they never said what the investigation was about. I didn't know then how much my life was going to change in such a short time.

Around the Christmas season, I went to visit my family in L.A. When I got back from L.A. my girlfriend picked me up from the airport and I noticed things felt a little different.

Something wasn't right. My girlfriend was angry because she didn't see me for over a week and wanted to spend time with me. I stayed in L.A. longer than I planned and we argued about it. The next morning, we got ready for school like we always did and left at the same time. As we made our way downstairs to our cars, I noticed three men with police officers behind them coming my way. They approached us and one of the officers asked if my name was Ralph Sanders. I replied "Yes" without thinking that they were looking for me or that I was in any kind of trouble. I truly thought they had the wrong person and this was all a mistake. How blind could I be? Without hesitation, the cop pulled my girlfriend away from me and told me to turn around. He handcuffed me and told me they would tell me what this was all about in the car. As it turned out, this man was the Stanford detective and he had Palo Alto cops with him. My girlfriend was crying so much and had no clue what had just happened. As the police car drove off, I felt such confusion. I began crying myself because I felt like we had just been ripped apart.

They took me to the Stanford campus jail and held me there for questioning. I hadn't been booked into the Palo Alto jail yet because they were still trying to determine if I was the guilty guy who was committing these thefts. They were building their case and I was running my mouth! This hurt me in the long run. I was so naive about it all! I had never been to jail and didn't realize I needed an attorney until later.

I was finally booked into the county jail in Palo Alto. What a cold and creepy place this was! There were guys in there that had absolutely no respect for one another. They were loud and nasty people to say the least. I remember feeling confined within the concrete walls that surrounded my view. I just wanted to make my one phone call so badly. They rolled this phone line down from cell to cell and we could only call collect. I had such a difficult time remembering numbers. We weren't allowed to have anything in there with us and my contacts were in my wallet. I called my girlfriend, but sadly, she wouldn't accept any of my calls. I was heartbroken. I was in that jail for four months and fighting my case most of the time. People who'd trusted me were furious about what I had done.

Loneliness set in and I began talking about my case with the other inmates. They told me they saw my story in the paper, which talked about a man who was going around and stealing stuff from the Stanford dormitories. The inmates I talked to were very negative and told me I was going to prison. They told me, "Hey man, you stole stuff from Stanford students! Have you lost your mind?! You are a brother and they don't like that you were stealing from 'their' students! They are going to wash you up for this one!" Other inmates were a little more positive. They thought I would get a break since it was my first offense and that I would only get probation.

At my arraignment in court, the charges were read to me. Seven felonies and seven forgeries! I was facing eight years max for my crimes! Eight years! This was my first offense! I chose to plead "not guilty" at this hearing. A public defender was appointed to me, but I had no idea how this process worked. After my brother was told by the public defender that I was fighting eight years in prison, he raised cash to get me a private attorney in Palo Alto. She seemed good and extremely convincing. She told me that she thought she could get some of the charges reduced. At my preliminary hearing, there were many students and bank tellers in the courtroom. The district attorney had all the witnesses subpoenaed to the hearing to help cement the charges against me. Since I had a private attorney, I thought she would be able to get probation for me. It didn't turn out the way I thought it would. I remember talking with the judge in his chambers, and he told my attorney that I should take the four years the D.A. recommended. Four years in prison? Was he out of his mind? I didn't want to go to prison, so I declined the plea bargain. I trusted my attorney, especially since she knew one of the judges who she wanted to hear the case. She recommended I have a court trial, which would mean waiving a jury trial and having a judge make the decision about my case. She reassured me it was a good idea because the judge would take my case home and study it thoroughly. She said she was friends with this judge and told me "don't worry" because I might get a joint suspension when I went on a 90-day observation visit to prison, and they would likely put me on probation afterward. Judgment Day arrived. I sat in the courtroom at Santa Clara Superior Court in San Jose. The judge told us to stand as he read all the charges. He found me guilty on all counts and set sentencing for a later date. This judge, my attorney's supposed friend, gave me five years in prison! This was one of the saddest days of my life. I had no idea what I was up against. For about four days, I remained in the county jail until I was transferred. I was learning a hard lesson. This was the point to become a man.

3

Imprisoned

It's 4 a.m. in June of 1990. I am sound asleep and I hear keys jangling. There's a loud voice yelling, "Get up, Sanders! It's that time!" I was going to prison today. Prison! I was in tremendous shock, but the reality of this situation was beginning to hit me. We had to strip down and take everything off. "Get in line and lean against the wall! Strip everything off...now! Throw your clothes on the floor in front of you." Orders are thrown at me.

They want to see if I am hiding anything on my body. "Run your fingers through your hair, Sanders... Put your hands in the air... Stick out your tongue and lift it up." But I was most degraded when they told me, "Turn around and lift your right foot first and wiggle your toes. Now the left...bend over and cough. Spread your cheeks, Sanders, open them as you cough three times." I never felt so degraded in my life. "Cough, cough, cough." Evidently, I wasn't doing it right and one of the guards that was going to be driving the bus to prison was infuriated because I wasn't doing it right. Some of the other inmates were on a parole violation and heading back to prison. This meant they had been through this process and had likely done this many times before.

There was so much going through my mind at this time that I was in a state of humbleness and could not feel the pain yet. We were chained up like animals, one next to the other. It reminded me of an image of slavery and the movie *Roots*. Many thoughts were spinning in my head. I was overwhelmed and began thinking about what a bad person I had become. I felt so out of place and didn't have a clue about how to talk with the inmates chained on either side of me. Chains hung from our torso and ankles. We were chained so close that we could barely walk and had to take baby steps to make our way to this large, green, and nasty dark-tinted window bus known as the "Gray Goose."

The Gray Goose was well known because it traveled all around the prisons in California. The Goose came equipped with three guards known as the transportation guards, who carried lots of weapons. These two would ride up front, while another guard sat in a cage in the back. That guard was the one with the attitude. He was an intimidating man and told us, "There will be no talking on this bus! If you want to talk with your neighbor, you have to lean next to him and whisper in his ear. This goes for everyone! You got that?" All of the guards wore dark shades just like in the movies. The transportation guards in the front were playing sad songs on the radio. I know it made some of us want to tear up. This was true for me because I started thinking about the happy times in my past, but I couldn't show others my tears, as it is a sign of weakness. Other inmates will interpret it as being "soft" and try to con you into doing things. This is something that was confirmed to me in prison.

I'd never felt so uncomfortable in my life. Riding on the Goose in a paper suit with nothing on underneath. The suits were made out of material that would tear easily. Mine did not fit me due to my large-sized body. My genitals were visible because when I sat down, the suit would tear wide open. But the guards didn't care. They didn't have an ounce of sympathy for any of us. To them, we were all criminals and not their friends. To make things worse, there was no bathroom on this bus. If it took five hours to get there, you just had to hold it until they made a gas stop, which was in the middle of nowhere where others could not see us. I began to realize I was a long way from home and from everybody. The sun is shining and it's a beautiful summer day as the bus makes its way through the city of San Francisco. I find it amazingly ironic that such a gorgeous view can be seen from inside of such an ugly contraption—the Gray Goose. Thoughts of what happened to me are going through my head as I try to understand how I even got here. At this point, I still don't have a clue why I am headed to San Quentin State Prison. It is extremely quiet. The music has been shut off and no one is talking. I hear the smooth ride of the wheels and notice the bars on the outside of the windows. The glass is so dark that no one can see us. I feel so lonely knowing that we have been extricated from society. As we begin to cross the Golden Gate Bridge, the inmates begin to stir and peer out the window to see one of the most beautiful sights in the world!

This is my thought because I have never been to this part of the city and had never crossed the Golden Gate Bridge. Sadness overwhelms me because beneath the bridge, I see people sailing in boats and riding on the ferry. Life is going on for them. I think to myself, that should be me out there with my girlfriend, riding on one of those boats and telling her how much I love her. I felt a dichotomy going on inside of me—sadness, yet an appreciation for the beauty before my eyes. The bus ride was numbing, as I didn't know what to feel on the Gray Goose. As we got closer to San Quentin and the many roads leading to it, I realized we were trapped, completely surrounded by the bay on two ends. Again I think, Such a beautiful view from within such an ugly place. As the bus pulls up to the front gate, the fear of the unknown engulfs my body. The inmate chained to my right reassures me, "You will be okay." Turns out, he was in for murder and got ten years. Why did I get so much time when I didn't even hurt anyone? I thought to myself; I couldn't hurt a fly. The bus stopped and the guards got out, including the guard in the back. It was then that everyone started talking because we were the only ones on the bus. We were all chained up and caged in the middle of the bus. We can't do anything until they come back to unlock us. As I look out the window, I can see the guards putting their guns up in a small building connected to the wall gate ready for us as we enter the prison. The guy next to me said, "There are no guns allowed in the prison. Only the guards can have them in the tower." I asked why and he replied, "Inmates can take guards over and take their guns, so they are not allowed on the grounds at all in any prison." I thought to myself, How can that be? I just didn't understand. What if I needed to be protected from fights or gangs?

The guards got back on the bus and one guard came on first and did a head count on the bus and then got off. We drove through these huge gates to this dreadful-looking prison. I begin feeling cold and my hands are now sweaty and clammy. The guards are looking tired, as if they have been doing this all day. We pull up to "Receiving and Release" (hereafter R&R), which is also known as R&R. This is where the prisoners are processed. As the bus pulls around the building to the lower yard, I can see the inmates working out. I think to myself, Oh my God! These guys are big and scary looking! They are all watching intently as the bus pulls up—as if they had never seen one come through.

"Stand up!" the guards ordered. "No talking to anyone outside the bus in the lower yard." One by one, we are brought to a cage in this building that is just a few steps away from the bus. Inmates are yelling at us and a couple of black guys are yelling, "Hey cuz! Where you from, homie?" I didn't know what to think or other races were shouting the same thing. Some of the guys on the bus already knew some of the inmates that were yelling at them. "Hey Wood! Welcome back! I have a pack of cigarettes for you!" I think to myself, This is his home and he was sent back. All the inmates are separated in the yard, sectioned off by race. This is difficult for me because I am diverse, and I hope we can talk with other people that are of a different race. I think, We haven't even had any breakfast and now we're in this huge cage. There are five of these cages that hold inmates who are going home, those that are going to court, and some who are just getting in like us! "New fish" is what we call it. I was a big one—green behind the eyes and ears of this walk of prison life. One by one, we are stripped down. We are given a disgusting bag lunch that holds a peanut butter sandwich, a small apple, and a small milk, just like the one we used to get in elementary school—except it's so nasty that I just can't eat it. Finally, after waiting for what seems like hours, at 1:00 p.m. our prison numbers are finally read out loud to us. "E-76192 SANDERS!"

After stepping back into the cage, our mug shots are taken. We are all classification inmates and will not be put on main line like the other inmates, at least not for three weeks until some of us can see a counselor. Soon we will be assigned to a unit or building and others will be shipped to other prisons on the point system. We are each given a rolled-up towel containing two boxers, two socks, a roll of toilet paper, white soap, and a small toothbrush the size of your pinky finger! This stuff is like something I have never seen! They put us all in orange jumpsuits, which is what we are going to be wearing until we get out of the West Block Reception Center.

As we walk to West Block on the upper yard, we have to pass deathrow inmates. Death row was located in North Block, which is one of the huge buildings on the upper yard. Death-row inmates are segregated from regular population. I remember seeing a caged door and reading on the top of it, "Condemned Row."

As we approach the basketball courts, some of the inmates are playing ball and arguing at the same time. Others on the sideline are looking at me saying, "You play that ball, my brother?" and yelling, "We will shoot you a kite when you get to the reception center. I will have one of the runners get at you." In prison, I learned that information is written on rolled-up paper called kites to communicate. These are passed down from one inmate to another.

This place is humongous—tall black doors separate every wing. Walking through West Block is overwhelming. This place is loud, crazy, and trashy. We are taken to our tiers and I am on the fifth tier. They have wire over the tiers because people were tossed off in the old days. There are holes in the walls and ceiling as I proceed down the tier all the way to the end. This is my new home for the next five years. As I pass through, there are inmates who want to talk and give me stuff to pass off to the next cell. Everyone is locked up as I walk by. There is a guard at the beginning of the tier watching me walk to my cell. By opening one handle, the guard unlocks all the cells at the same time. As I stand in front of my cell, holding my roll of stuff, the guard yells, "Cell block door open! Stay inside!" As I walk in, the cell locks right behind me. There's a guy asleep in the cell. He jumps up and says, "Hey Celly, what's your name, brother?" I sat there and did not move. First of all, the cells are the size of my current walk-in closet and I can reach the ceiling and touch the top. I replied, "My name is Ralph." He says to me, "You play ball or something, Celly?" I began to tell him my story and he stopped me and said, "Don't tell anyone your story, Celly." Even though I told him my name, he kept calling me "Celly." He said there are a lot of people in here that you can't trust even though they seem trustworthy. Don't discuss your case with anyone. People are conniving and full of hate, especially when they know you're going home before them. As I hear him talking to me, I realize he was a lifer and he was not telling me what he was in for—we got off that subject real fast. I could spread my hands out and touch both walls of the cell width-wise. The toilet is in the corner where we lay are heads, and it is a steel toilet that turns cold when you sit on it. The sink is connected to the toilet.

The cell walls have writing all over them, including gang writing. I can clearly see the time of other inmates before me who kept track of their days in this cell. This cell is the most disgusting thing. On the walls, there is dried-up snot, dried-up food, and pictures of a sexual nature. My new cellmate gave me the top bunk. I was very uncomfortable. My feet hung over the top and I always had to climb up there. I had to put my feet on his bunk to get to my bed. It was really hot at times. I could touch the ceiling with the palm of my hand. We were so confined in here. We are allowed to leave our cells only twice a day. We are let out for breakfast and dinner, and we line up for both. If you don't wake up in time for breakfast, you will miss the nasty lunch they pass them out in the chow line after breakfast. I am escorted and at times I can see death-row inmates being escorted to the hospital located in the prison for dental work or whatever they needed. We have to face the wall or sit down when they escort anyone from high-power custody. High-power custody are death-row inmates and inmates that are coming from the Hole. The Hole is part of the prison where inmates are locked up for being involved in riots, stabbings, and assaults on the C.O.'s, or Correctional Officers (hereafter C.O.'s).

The next day my "bunkie" was going to be transferred to another prison where they keep high-custody inmates because of the life term he had to do. He already saw classification and they endorsed him to

Corcoran Level Four Prison, where Charles Manson has been held for decades. We talked about his transfer tomorrow, and he related that he was excited to get out of West Block and start his time. I thought to myself, *Life, wow!* This guy was in and out of prison because he knew lots of people and knew the ropes around this place. He was way too informed about things and how to do time. My cellmate was picked up early in the morning around 4 a.m. I woke up and he was gone!

For the first time in months, I now find myself alone and able to think about my situation. Feelings of profound sadness overcome me and I am crying to myself, secretly wishing I hadn't committed the forgeries. Being alone in this closed space, I am able to finally release my emotions and just cry. I hear the inmate in the cell next to me say, "Hey brother! Where you from?" I wonder, Did he hear me sobbing? I am somewhat hesitant to say anything back, but I reply, "My name is Ralph." This inmate told me, "It's all good—you won't be in this place for too long, maybe just a couple more weeks. They may keep you here or send you out. He explained that this is the hard part because there's no access to the yard, no church, no visits, no phones, and no talking with others. We are here for the reception center to classify us and find out where we will be transferred next. The process is painstaking because there are so many prisoners to be processed. For instance, in my building alone, there are about 5,000 inmates on all the tiers. Each of us has to be fed and classified. The number is horrendous.

After coming back from the chow line, we are escorted in a long line back to West Block. We have to get ready for our weekly shower. Yes, that's right, weekly, as in one time per week! The tiers are punished sometimes for other inmates' bad behavior, and we only get one shower a week. Some of the inmates act up and give the C.O.'s a hard time, like catcalling a female guard or saying, "Hey, Girl!" It's practically impossible to tell what cell the catcall is coming from so it ruins access to showers for that entire tier. I hate West Block and the fact that we never get out of our cells for nothing more than chow!

When we are let out for showers, the inmates run down the stairs to get a spot in the showers because we only have three minutes to shower! This is such a short time even if you're only getting wet, much less soaping up and rinsing off! If we want that shower, we need to be ready and waiting to dash out of our cells when the gates crack open. Seems that every kind of person is in prison. There's even what we call a "he-she" in prison. A "he-she" is a person who has convincing-looking female breasts and a butt, but is male. They even act as a woman would.

They entice the other inmates to look at them. I found myself looking because I could not believe what I was seeing in the shower. There's no doubt that this place is a different walk of life.

After a month in West Block, I am finally seeing my counselor. It's refreshing knowing that I get to sit on the yard for five hours to shoot the breeze, talk the jive, and play basketball, but most of all watch the seagulls fly over the prison. There is seagull crap everywhere. After some time, I finally get called into the office. My counselor tells me she is going to endorse me to do my time here at San Quentin.

She says I should be getting out of West Block in a couple of weeks.

As time goes on, I have a new bunkie who is an inmate from East Oakland. He's a cool guy who has filled me in on the rules of survival in prison. Turns out that he is a repeat offender for the seventh time! He is here for robbery and doing seven years. He told me how to survive and stay "sucker free." The rules to follow so you get out of here alive are: 1. You don't borrow. 2. You don't steal. 3. You don't mess with gays. 4. You don't share too much information about yourself. I didn't get it until later and had to see for myself. Prison rules were something I had to learn on my own over time.

"Sanders! E-76192!" My name was called over the loudspeaker. All inmates that will be housed in the prison on mainline are moving on! I have been waiting for this over 56 days and they finally called my name along with several other inmates. We are all packing and getting our meager possessions to get out of West Block. In ten minutes, they are going to be popping my cell open. "Good luck on the line, homie!" my bunkie exclaimed. "Thanks," I say. "Take care of yourself." Walking out of my cell, I pass inmates in their cells that want me to pass stuff to other cells. I find that it's very loud in here because after chow time and showers, the inmates get bored. It's much like a game crowd of voices penetrating the whole building. I say to myself, *I got to go, homie, just keep walking.* There's a guard standing at the end of the tier waiting for me. In my mind, I have no idea about where I'm going, but it has to be a better place than this.

The guard is telling me they are taking me to another part of the prison called CARSON section, otherwise known as "C" Block. It is ugly and the steps in that place are creepy. After entering the building, they change me into prison blues and shoes. I am not talking basketball shoes...these are Bubba Gump converse P.I.A. (Prison Industry Authority) shoes! Many of the cells are open and people are programming (following the rules of the C.O.'s program rather than the rules of the convicts) and standing on the tiers and talking. I see radios, 13-inch TV's, CD players, and books. There are inmates who are wearing crosses and gold chains. People are walking and talking in low tones. All of the phones downstairs are being used. These guys look content, as if they are just living their lives here, doing time. This is the main line. This is about to become the beginning of my lesson learning and a time for me to really grow up fast!

Walking past one person's cell to get to mine on the second tier, I see an inmate who has everything in his cell—you name it, he's got it. Things like food as well as material things. I see two black guys exchanging a box of cigarettes for a box of top ramen soup. They are making a deal. One of the guys asks me if I need mps to write my family. I certainly do! This guy is called the stamp man because he has lots of stamps and everyone has their own hustle. He is going to deal with me later after breakfast because they are locking us up for night yard. I don't want to go to night yard because I'm not ready to face the yard yet. The breeze from the water is cold and I just want to be alone for a week or so. I am starting to feel really depressed and sick to my stomach. What I am seeing is making me feel so out of place. I feel homesick and need to see a psychiatrist for an interview so I can take something to get me out of this mood. I have been feeling this way for many weeks now. I find that when they let us out for chow to walk and get our food, I feel better at times but always out of place.

In the kitchen, there are huge paintings, like murals, on the walls. We can sit down in the chow hall for a mere ten minutes to finish our food, but then we must walk back to our cells immediately after that. I am trying to get used to the food because it's so bad. The dinners are okay and we are served well-balanced meals. I can see why homeless people like it in this place now! Free room and board, I guess.

Walking back to my cell, I see reception inmates being escorted sometimes. Looking back, I remember it was worse there than where I am now. I still haven't made a phone call or written a letter home in almost three months. I finally got my first phone call today after being in "C" Block over three weeks because you can't use the phone without a "C" Block prison ID on you. I am so excited to make a call. The first person I tried calling was my girlfriend, who I just needed to forget about. I was in love, or maybe I was just so lonely that I needed to hear her voice. She won't accept the call. I called my sister next and she answered! The phone kept beeping every minute because the prison phones record the entire conversation. My sister is concerned about me. I put my head down and started crying and told her I needed to get out of here. There are so many things I need from her so I ask, "Would you please send me cash for my books, paper for writing, and stamps? And pictures of you and the family? Would you also please call my attorney and find out the status of my appeal? Oh! And I can't remember my brothers' numbers and I want to call them. Please call my girlfriend for me, too!"

I am so frustrated because there are so many things I want but can't have right now. The ten-minute phone call was so short because I cried most of the time. I was careful not to let anyone see me crying because it is taken as a sign of weakness. I just walked back to my cell and lay there and thought to myself, How can I get another phone call? We are allowed one call every other day for inmates on the second floor, and these have to be collect calls. The other inmates are calling me the "Stressor" because I need to use the phone all the time. These guys watch and see everything in here. Nobody misses a thing.

Other inmates are able to have visitors. As they are being called for visits, I notice how nice they look in their brand-new blues. I am envious as I see them lined up at the door on the first floor to receive their passes to walk through the upper yard for visiting. The rules are that I can't receive any visitors until my family sends in a visiting form. The process can take up to 90 days while CDC does background checks and investigates who is coming to visit. If my family could only come and visit me! I miss them immensely. I have to get stamps from that guy who is trading them for food and other stuff! I see him walking around on every tier saying, "Stamps for sale...stamps for sale!" I told him I needed a couple and he said, "Well I need at least three top ramen soups, you got chicken?" I told him that I hadn't made the store yet and I was on third draw. The stamp man said, "Brother, that's in eight days and I don't know if I can swing that!" I told him I was desperate to write home and I would get the soups to him when I made the draw for canteen next week. "Oh, okay, my brother. I will look for it next week. How many do you need?" "Just four," I replied. "I got you." Everything costs around here but we get free blank paper. Finally, I am able to write to my family! I finally got to see the psych in medical to tell him how I've been feeling. He put me on antidepressants and Thorazine pills. This is very heavy medication. These pills make me feel lethargic and my mouth is watery all the time. I am on this stuff because I am always depressed and can't take the cell living.

About four months has passed since I've been on this block. I am starting to have issues with the stamp guy because he wants his stamps. In the yard, when I was watching the inmates play ball, he walked up to me with two other inmates and said, "If you don't give me back my 8 stamps, you will owe me 12! That's interest after being late more than two weeks, nigga!" The stamp man is not happy, and I am not thinking right because I am drugged up and just don't care. My habits from the streets hurt me because one day I was on the tier ready for chow. The stamp guy was approaching me and walked right past me and did not say anything to me. I wanted to tell him, "They are coming in the mail this week. My sister just sent 30 stamps," but I didn't say anything. On the way back from chow, I was sitting by myself. Sometimes the guys sit with me and I think it's kind of strange. I didn't know I had a hit out on me! As we walk back, it's always crowded as we walk to our cells because there are so many inmates passing through. All of a sudden, I feel something hard go in my side and someone saying, "You late, nigga!" It hurt really badly and I fell to the floor. Blood was coming from my blues and there I was lying on the second floor. "Man down!" someone shouted. I hear keys jingling and getting closer to me. I am feeling dizzy and "out of it." I am quickly taken on a gurney to the medical department. I almost lost my life over a couple of stamps!

4

Baptized in "H" Unit

The doctors patched me up and sent me back to main line after just two days in the hospital. I didn't stay in "C" Block too long. My points were going down and my counselor liked the fact that I was not the typical inmate. My points dropped so I was allowed to go outside the walls of the prison to do my remaining time. It was a better place but it would be a little while longer, about four months, before that happened. I hated the fact that I had to live in a small cell and that it was making me go nuts. I couldn't think right being depressed all the time. I had to see the psychiatrist once again, who put me on so many meds that my walking was inhibited, not to mention my issues were a blur. I was taking the meds before I got stabbed, but the doctor ordered more in order to decrease the stress on my body. After getting stabbed, I came to the realization that I needed to "wake up" and stop feeling sorry for myself. I realized that no one in this godforsaken place would take care of me except me. The meds were more than my body could take. I wanted to be in the right mind. So I asked to be taken off the medication. During these nights I cried and I prayed, and I prayed some more.

I began reading this little Bible I was given. I'd never really looked in one of them before in my entire life. But that week I started reading it out of desperation and fear. I was looking for direction because no one was going to take care of me in jail. I was on my own. Most inmates simply focus on their release date and their program. However, I decided to follow God's word that said, "Be still and know that I am God" (Psalms 46:10). It's all about right choices. I never wanted to listen to God before because I didn't know him. Just like I didn't know that guy who put me in the hospital by stabbing me. Had I known I would get hurt, I never would have borrowed anything from anyone. I remembered the guy from West Block who told me the rules, and to never borrow was one of them. He told me, "Before you take anything from anyone here, make sure you know them and what they are about!"

I stayed in the hospital for what seemed like an eternity. The hospital was a quiet place for two days, and I had a lot of time to myself lying there in that bed. I started reading, and falling asleep while reading. I felt as if God was talking to me. I wasn't sure who it was, but over time I built a relationship with something! Someone else started doing the talking for me rather than myself. I had a lot of expectations from reading the Word because I wanted to be out of prison and to be one step closer to freedom. I still carried a negative attitude as my soul waited silently for God alone to move me where I needed to be. But it never occurred to me, or I had a hard time resonating in my heart, that this was where God wanted me at that moment. I didn't want to believe it because I thought I was different and didn't belong in prison. I didn't want to think this way, but I was a hypocrite, a liar, and I was trying to hustle myself through life. God wanted to encounter me and help me to realize that I didn't have to hustle anymore.

The following week I was housed in a place called "H" Unit. H Unit is located right outside the walls of San Quentin. The barracks are all the places in the yard where you were to be housed. Since my points lowered to just 20 points, I was qualified to be considered for level one custody. I was eligible for the "ranch"—the place they keep lower custody inmates. It was dormitory style living. Big difference, Thank God! It was much more spacious and we were able to move around more freely. The C.O.'s are calling names from the building. I prayed they would call me. After 14 or 15 names they said my name. Praise God! Yes! I was off to pack the few possessions I had—a bedroll and toothbrush. We were escorted to our new home for the next three years. Oh, how I was eager with anticipation to get to the other side of this wall. People told me we were going to do fine there and complete our program with no issues because most inmates there had a release date. We had something to look forward to. Lifers hardly ever reach low custody. Watching the towers and the way they handle the keys are so creepy. It made me feel like I was a bad person, knowing everything and knowing how everyone was locked up. You always needed to either open or lock something or someone up. A bucket is dropped down from the tower on a string. There's a key inside that opens the gate which leads to "H" Unit.

"H" Unit contains dorms numbered 1 through 15. "H Unit" was definitely a different world. However, it housed the same people and the same prison mentality! It reminded me of what a concentration camp or boot camp would be like.

Being in "H" Unit was a little easier than inside the walls of the main prison. However, looking at the ugly high walls, towers, and buildings made me feel like I was still in prison. I was feeling a little different in this place, but the reality of prison rules was still going on around me, with the rules and crazy stuff. I was put in dorm 13 and later moved to other dorms. You could move at times if you did not like your dorm. "H" Unit was the place where I spent most of my five-year sentence.

Serving good time with no trouble allowed me a reduced sentence. Instead of five years, I got to serve three and a couple of months.

After getting stabbed I did not want any more issues. The word got to my side of the prison that I was stabbed and people would come over all the time to visit. People passed the word down that I was stabbed. In prison there is an unwritten rule that nothing should be spoken about. I started playing basketball quite a lot, exercising and working out. I was off the medication in an open environment where I could deal with my situation better. I started looking healthier (although the food wasn't so great); I was taking care of myself. Church was something that helped me and I clung to it. It was helpful to read the Bible with other people. However, I had to remember where I was—in prison—and some inmates were not to be trusted. Unfortunately, I was in a world of criminals; I was one of them. I attended church every Sunday morning and Bible study Tuesday nights. I became really involved, which encouraged me to feel very remorseful for the crime that landed me in prison. I was baptized the following month and was happy to become a born-again Christian. That month I renewed my commitment to Christ. "Therefore, if anyone is in Christ, he is a new creation; old things have passed away; behold, all things have become new" (2 Corinthians 5:17). I committed myself to being a full-time Christian.

I tried my best to hang with saints that were part of the Bible study groups because they usually stayed out of harm's way. In prison there is no way you can just hang by yourself; everyone needs somewhere to belong. I remember playing ball against "Goliath" and his buddies. They always won the games, kicking all of us off court. No one could beat them. There was a basketball summer league and all the inmates were waiting to see if the "new guy" could play. *I was that new guy!* I was put on one of the teams—let's not forget, these were not your normal basketball players. They were more like "five to life" basketball players. I told myself I would not get involved, but giving my all at a moment like this would help to make my prison time go faster. People stood around and watched to see if we were going to beat "Goliath and the crew." We did! However, this was hurtful to the big guy's image. I threatened him with my talents and his homeboys were mocking him as I took advantage of him on the court. At the same time, I didn't consider how this could be a bad idea, especially with "Goliath" in the picture. I didn't know he was a shot caller/gang member from East Palo Alto—the bay area. What happened next was crazy. When the game was over, my teammates thanked me but Goliath walked up to me, punched me, and walked away. I didn't know what that was all about, but later that night he came storming in my dorm with four other guys. With gloves on he walked right up to my bunk. I was reading the Bible on my bunk. He snatched me up off the bunk. He was about 6'7", same height as me. He was very aggressive and looked like a thug. They all had their jackets and work gloves from yard crew on. Who knows what they had under their jackets? Were they going to shank me, stab me, and beat me down? Well, they beat me down and punched me into the shower room.

Since the prison code includes an anti-snitch mentality where everyone minds their own business, no one is supposed to tell on one another because you don't want a "snitch on your jacket," meaning you don't want to report anything on paper. It is a real serious violation of the prison code—you can get killed for letting the guards know about any violations involving other inmates. These guys circled me in the bathroom with five toilets, eight sinks, and grotesque dorm floors. They beat me up bad even though I tried to fight back. The big man, Goliath, was punching me and all I remember seeing was stars. My legs gave out and I fell down. One of the guys from my dorm got me up and washed the blood off my face and from the left side of my leg. My chest was hurting so bad that I could hardly walk. My eye was busted and quickly swelling up fast. This happened right before "dorm recall," where they make an announcement over the intercom for everyone to report to their bunks for head count.

Count time was always at 4:00 p.m. When count was over we would get ready for all the dorms to walk to chow one at a time (it's not like I could walk to chow). When the correctional officers walk by for count, they want to see your body and face. Luckily, they did not see my eye because it felt huge. If they had seen my face, they would have brought me into the office to file a report and try to get information on who did it. Then they would write you up thinking you had a fight, and I could have received 30 extra days in prison. I could have told, but I didn't want to be considered a snitch as it would hurt me in the long run. I always considered protective custody, but you have to be in the main prison for that. Plus, it's worse because you have very little yard time and it's a small world. Everyone in Protective Custody (hereafter PC), like child molesters and etc., all have a "bad jacket." I did not want that "jacket" on me. A jacket is basically a negative reputation that makes others view you as a sellout; it is like you have a "hit" out on you if you have a "bad jacket." In protective custody there are a lot of snitchers, gang dropouts, those who may have told on their homeboys, or one who'd reported fights. One thing good in PC is that you serve time without many issues (I guess). I've never been there and I guess it was not God's calling for me. I would see these guys on the court, but I stopped playing ball and just continued to go to church and shoot by myself at times when no one was around. There were only two courts broken down by race on different days throughout the week. Politics were still prevalent on the yard.

After a year and a half of "H" Unit, in the middle of the day on a Saturday afternoon, they called me for a visit and I thought it was another Sanders they had a mix-up with! Well that's me, and I had no clue who could have been there to see me. After getting all ready, I went to the visiting room for the first time after almost two years of being in prison. I tried to look my best because this was like going out someplace nice. There are over 120 people from the streets in the visiting area. There are lots of women, children, and normal people having a good time visiting family, eating the good food from the vending machines, and enjoying a day out of prison. They pat you down at the door and let you in when you show them your ID.

Wow! I could not believe who I was looking at! It was my ex-girlfriend from Stanford. I hugged her right away and she did the same. It was a feeling I can't explain. I was numb by the fact that she was standing right there in front of me. She was crying and kept hugging me and telling me she was sorry that this was happening to me. I kept telling her, "It's okay and I forgive you."

We talked about what was going on with her and how she graduated with honors in biology from Stanford. She had been living in Sacramento and I had never been there before. She came every Saturday and Sunday for visits over the rest of my time. What a surprise! We decided to get married, and once we did we began having conjugal visits.

She was a godsend. At my major time of suffering God brought me company, comfort, and romance. I needed all those things. What a relief it was to do just that! When we talked about getting married, after visiting for over six months, we grew tired of merely kissing, holding hands, and talking for six hours in the visiting room. We always thought of the desire wanting to be alone and express our love for one another. So out of nowhere, we started talking about getting married right in the visiting room. The prison chaplain came in and married us right in the back of the room. It was not a special ceremony except that we exchanged rings and enjoyed our visit. We would have to wait until the following month for our conjugal visits to start; we were both really excited. Conjugal visits were a way to pass time without stress and to get away from the prison. I would walk back in the prison after stripping down and go back to my dorm with the knowledge that I had support through a wife with a place to parole to. I was so happy we had family visits the next month after marriage and would be able to have sex and spend time to talk about life. I really hoped we worked out. In the following two weeks, I was moved to the Ranch outside the gates of "H" Unit. This was great! "The Ranch" was the lowest custody area one could get, and I was placed on the Caltrans crew. This orange van would pick us up and we'd hit the city with a twelve-man crew. Our job was cleaning trash off the freeways; clean-up in the city of Marin, California, and other places. I was blessed to serve out the rest of my time at the Ranch rather than "H" Unit. We stayed in cubicles and each had our own 13-inch amongst other things. It was like staying in barracks; we could walk to chow out of order and go as we pleased. It was better than H Unit because I had more control rather than being controlled more. Everyone had less than two years of time remaining.

I recall longer visits with my wife. Visiting was nice because we could sit outside and talk and enjoy the sun. We would take walks along the grass and kiss and hold each other tight. They would lock us in this yard with gates surrounding it. There were six other little trailers, and there was grass and a playground in the middle for children. We got to walk outside anytime and spend time in this little world gated up for three days. I was so thankful to have this in my time of suffering. I felt like Daniel in the lion's den when the angel of the Lord shut the lion's mouth and they went to sleep. Instead of devouring Daniel, the lions were at peace and did not harm him. The same was for me. I was in a prison den, but the lion's did not devour me. It seemed that we weren't watched as closely, but the guards were still taking their walks and making sure nothing was going on like breaking the rules. The conjugal visits were great to have, but I was always sad when they were over. It seemed like I was out of prison but was quickly brought back to reality every time they would count us in. We had to do count time at the same time every time no matter what we were in the middle of.

Since I was really close to getting out, I began putting my parole plans together. When you are thirty days to getting out you get a "ducket" called "S" time. A "ducket" means that you are no longer ordered to report to work so you have a lot of time to get things together. With a ducket you can call, getting your "dress outs," which are civilian clothes to wear for being released.

I also attended a pre-release program inside the walls every day. I got my license, Social Security card, and information about potential jobs. The pre-release program was inside the prison, so of course I was escorted every day. I was escorted every time inside the prison because that's where the program was located. I was able to find some helpful information, but my wife did most of the work.

The day had finally come! It was time for me to go home! I was so ready to get out of this place that nothing was going to stop me. I had to sit in R&R along with the other inmates who were released on parole as well. The process reminded me of when I came into this place and how the process seemed endless. There I was—sitting in the huge tank with other inmates who were talking trash, like how they were going to get drunk or get laid or get some drugs when they got out. Some were positive, but others were negative. I just wanted out. Whoever had a ride out front would get dropped off in the same place where that nasty "Grey Goose" bus had brought us in. Others without rides had to get dropped off by the prison van to the nearest Greyhound or train station. It is a law you cannot be walking near the prison grounds as a parolee. The sun was rising as I walked out of the front gate. It was a beautiful day, and I recall looking at my wife on the other side of the gate from a distance. As I reached her with my bag in hand, I talked with the CO's, who told me, "Don't come back, Sanders!" I responded, "I will never return! I have too much going on for me." He replied, "That's what they all say. You'll be back." He had a smile on his face like he was teasing me, but I knew he was giving me something to think about. We hugged and my wife and I walked over to the car.

Riding in this nice car with my new wife and crossing the Bay Bridge seemed strange to me. I was seeing life again and feeling free for the first time in five years. We stopped at the park on the other side of the bridge. In the park, there was a lovely pond with ducks paddling about. I remember we were the only ones in this park near the water. My beautiful wife had a picnic planned for us. I began crying because I had held my emotions in for so long. What happened to me was frightening, but I was blessed to make it out of that place. We drove to the city of Sacramento for the first time ever in my life. The city seemed small but my wife had a nice apartment. As we entered it, I saw pictures of us that my wife had framed. I began to weep all over again just like I did at the park. She had saved our letters and framed them. I thought to myself, She really loves me and really cares. I didn't have family there for me and no visits from anyone except her. It was amazing how she gave me a comfort zone to progress and grow without fail. I knew then that this was the work of God giving me the chance to rebuild what I had lost, giving me back what the devil stole. But I planned on making this time even better than before.

5

A Taste of Freedom

It seemed so nice to be near this beautiful pond surrounding the big houses and the apartment complex across the street. I was so happy to have been out and walking around this new place where I lived. My new home was located about 10 minutes from downtown Sacramento. It was a really nice area called the Greenhaven Pocket Area. It was where a lot of the Sacramento Kings' basketball players lived. I had to see my parole officer that following Monday since I was released on a Friday and the parole office was closed on the weekends. First thing Monday, I reported to the office to meet him for the first time. It was crazy because being there brought back memories of the inside world I'd just left. The people in the lobby were loud and talking like they do in the cage. I stayed to myself in the lobby. There were about 11 other people that were on parole also waiting to see their parole officers. A lot of the guys were talking bad about what the system didn't do for them. Some were saying things like "I hope they don't find out I am dirty." Dirty, as in he or she did drugs last night, as every month we had to be drug tested. I sat there while my wife waited in the car. I wanted her to come in with me so I called her to wait in the lobby with me so she could meet my parole officer. However, I was uncomfortable having her sit in the lobby with me with all that was going on with the other parolees. I thought to myself, "DO NOT BE CONFORMED TO THIS WORLD, BUT BE TRANSFORMED BY THE RENEWING OF YOUR MIND, THAT YOU MAY PROVE WHAT IS THE GOOD AND ACCEPTABLE AND PERFECT WILL OF GOD" (Romans 12:2).

While I was waiting, this one guy walked in and asked for his parole officer and immediately he was handcuffed and sent back to prison. My guess is that he was arrested on a parole violation. A cop car was outside waiting and the officer came right in and took him away. I never wanted that to happen to me.

Finally, after a few more minutes of waiting, my parole officer opened the door and said "Sanders." There he was...tall, heavy with a long beard and Afro—and he was black! I stood up and introduced him to my wife. We followed him to the back in his office and he opened my file. This file had everything on me like who I am and what I had done, as well as my parole release date and special conditions of parole. I had to follow those conditions and obey them to the "T"! My parole officer was kind of cool and asked me when I got married. I let him know that we were married in prison because my file didn't have that information. He said, "Wow! They got you for five years and it was only 1,100 dollars! You really pissed some people off and stepped on the wrong toes, Sanders. State your 'E' number for the record and that this is you. I will have to take a picture of you and a picture of the car that you drive. I will also get a house visit scheduled this week. Let's go over your conditions of parole and get you two out of here." I stated, "E-76192, Ralph I. Sanders." He walked me down the hallway and gave me a random drug test. I had to piss in the bottle and keep the bathroom door open as he watched me pee. I stated, "I don't do drugs." He said, "It's random for everyone on parole now. This is how it's going to be, Sanders, for the duration of your parole."

My conditions were that I couldn't leave town without him know-ing; I couldn't go 50 miles outside of my parole address without a pass from my parole officer; I had to report every first Monday of the new month; and he would call me for a house visit every month and I must be home during the visit. He was really shocked to see that I had done so much time for the charges of such a little amount of money. Sadness swept over me at that moment as I realized they could just cuff me and put me away at any time for any reason. According to my paperwork, I was going to be on parole for three long years. My release date was all I could think of every month that passed. I just kept working and doing the right thing. I never wanted to get a violation and go back. My plan was to stay out of trouble and do things right. My parole officer never came that week for the house visit and let me believe he would, I guess. What they do is pop up when you are not expecting them to come. Two weeks later on a Tuesday night we heard this loud knock on the door, and it was the parole officer with one of his partners. They didn't have guns showing but they had them. They were dressed in normal clothes and looked like undercover cops. They asked to come in because my wife opened the door. I could hear them from the bathroom. I came out into the living room where my parole officer was standing. He wanted to know where my room was so he could search it. He searched my closet, dresser, and under our bed. He looked around as he talked with us in a nice tone, reassuring us and saying, "This is normal routine, Sanders. Sometimes I won't call and if you're not home when I come over, I will just put my card on your door and you just give me a call." Wow, I thought to myself. It's going to be like this all the time. I didn't ask too many questions because I just wanted them to go away. He drug-tested me again and had me pee in this little bottle, all the while watching me do it. Oh my gosh! This was the second time in two weeks. I had a great attitude the whole time because God wants us to follow the laws and obey authority.

I remembered reading in Romans also about the laws of the land, which helped me get through the attitudes of all the people around me in prison, including the guards.

As a Christian, I wanted to follow the government and the laws. "LET EVERY SOUL BE SUBJECT TO THE GOVERNMENT AUTHORITIES, FOR THERE IS NO AUTHORITY EXCEPT FROM GOD, AND THE AUTHORITIES THAT EXIST ARE APPOINTED BY GOD" (Romans 13:1-3). My first month out was difficult finding work and getting things on track. I spent a lot of time working out because that was what I was accustomed to after all those years in prison. My wife and I attended this church called Capital Christian and started meeting a lot of really good people. This helped me to stay close to what I became and how I saw myself. I kept the vision. We attended church every Sunday. Church was a place of safety and away from bad company. I liked my new life and I still had a passion to play basketball. I was trying to get back into those things that would help me make a living out of it. I knew it would be hard after doing what I did and all that time I served, but I was still young—only 25—and had a chance to make something of myself, despite the bad choices I made in the past. "I CAN DO ALL THINGS IN CHRIST WHO STRENGTHENS ME" (PHILIPPIANS 4:13).

I stumbled on this job in downtown Sacramento working for valet parking at a really nice restaurant called Il Fornaio. It's an Italian restaurant located down the street from the beautiful capitol beneath the Wells Fargo Center that has 24 floors. I worked there for four months parking the employees' cars. I put my great people skills to use and earned excellent tips. One Friday night this guy and his girlfriend got out of this really nice convertible white classy CLK Mercedes-Benz. He was a little tipsy and told me, "You should be helping the Kings out!" I told him I wish I could but I had no connections but I played ball. He turned around and said, "What are you doing parking cars?" I said, "It's a long story and I would love to talk about it when you get some time one day, sir." He gave me his card and told me to call him. I told him I certainly would call him. I met a lot of wealthy people parking cars and soon learned this was a great spot to meet the people who have their lives together. Well, as a saint, it seemed to me that they did. Soon after, I was eating with my wife and she inquired how work was going. I told her all about how I met this guy who wants me to call him about work. I told her what happened and she asked who this guy was so I pulled out his business card from my pocket. He was running a couple of insurance companies from what I remember. I called him and we talked about basketball. We met down at his office, and he was on the 18th floor of the Wells Fargo Center. It was exciting to visit up there to talk with this man about something I had no clue about what! He was extremely interested in my ball skills and I told him my story. He happened to know the Kings' trainer, and one Saturday morning he picked me up in his beautiful car and brought me down to meet the Kings' trainer. Riding in this car with the top down on a beautiful summer Saturday morning, I thought to myself, I wonder what he wants from me. After all those years in prison, I learned that we don't get anything without giving something in return. I soon found out that he wanted to become my agent, and he took a liking to my spirit I would say. "LET BROTHERLY LOVE CONTINUE, DO NOT FORGET TO ENTERTAIN STRANGERS, FOR BY SO, DOING SOME HAVE UNWITTINGLY ENTERTAINED ANGELS" (Hebrews 13:1). He was like a godsend that day. I believe it was all in God's plan to happen that way.

We got out of his car in the huge parking lot at Arco Arena, now known as the Power Balance Arena, where the Kings were practicing inside. My new friend had a connection with them, and he was a friend with the trainer. We walked through security and right down to the locker room where I met the Kings' trainer. The players were training and Mitch Richmond, one of their good guards, walked right past me and said, "What's new?" I replied, "Checking it out" as we were walking to the trainer's office. I was interviewed and I had this tape of me that I brought.

They wanted to see it after I had already shown it to the man that brought me there. The trainer really liked the tape and had me start training with them the following day. This is where life began working well for me.

I was on the Sacramento Kings summer pro-team and trying to make the team. I was in training with them all summer long, hanging around the players and doing what I loved and what I always dreamed of doing. I was at practice every morning at the arena, and my wife would drop me off because we shared one car. I would usually get a ride home from one of the players that were already on the team like Mitch Richmond, Randy Brown, Wayman Tisdale, and other NBA players that I was training and hanging out with. I was not working at the time because I was in deep training and on my way to the tryouts for Sioux Falls Basketball CBA team in South Dakota. Their scouts discovered me for the South Dakota Sky Force basketball team. It was a sad day because I had to go home and tell my wife. We talked about it and it was a blessing. I got the chance to get invited to the CBA tryout the following month, and my parole officer let me go and it was great! He gave me a two weeks' pass and I would have to return or I could get a violation. It was hard for me to even have a clear mind in another state trying to make this team. It was all very bad...I got cut and had to come back and face the beginning that I started from.

I continued to stay in church and in good shape by always working out at the gyms and staying in touch with the players. I got to hang

out and go to functions and parties when invited. I always wanted to live the NBA lifestyle and have the things that I saw and dreamed of doing. This was something I enjoyed; I loved playing basketball. I started hanging out late and going to clubs and drinking and hanging out with the guys and doing what I thought was okay. My wife was not liking it as I was starting to fool around and do things that I knew I should not have done like lying and hiding things in my marriage and trying to be something I wasn't! "Lay aside all filthiness and overflow of wickedness, and receive with meekness the implanted word, which is able to save your souls" (James 1:21). Immediately, I forgot what kind of man I was. It seemed that bad company was the downfall of my marriage, and I started falling into the things that my heart was deceived to feel for. I could not keep myself unspotted from the world and its lusts. It seemed that I forgot all about the suffering and pain I went through to get so far. It was as if I was walking away from God; I was ignorant of God! "FRIENDSHIP WITH THE WORLD IS ENMITY WITH GOD" (James 4:4). Resist the devil and he will flee from you, but I was weak to resist and let the devil in. Rather than drawing near to God, I started drifting far away. A double-minded man is unstable in all his ways. I was missing days of fellowship and losing focus in my marriage and letting go of what was working for my new life out of prison. The Half-time Hustler was trying to creep back in. "DO NOT BE DECEIVED. EVIL COMPANY CORRUPTS GOOD HABITS. AWAKEN TO RIGHTEOUSNESS, AND DO NOT SIN; FOR SOME DO NOT HAVE THE KNOWLEDGE OF GOD" (1 Corinthians 15:33).

6

Slipping into Darkness

Things seemed to go nowhere with basketball and my marriage and faith. I started losing everything. At least I thought I was losing it all because my wife and I split up and went different ways. I wasn't faithful to her and didn't love her like I thought I did. I thought to myself that maybe she should have never come back by popping up in prison to visit me. I didn't know what I wanted out of this relationship, so we divorced and went our separate ways. I transferred my parole to L.A. and put in a 30-day notice to my parole officer. He made it happen and I was transferred to my sister's house in Carson, California. I had no choice but to be paroled there because you have to have a real address from family to do so. My sister wasn't happy with the fact that I was doing this but helped me get to L.A. to start my parole there. I was having a hard time in Sacramento with my parole officer after going through my divorce issue. Things were changing because she was my support, so I had to move and go back home. We never talked after our divorce. We lost contact and moved on with our lives. I never stayed at my sister's house even though it was my parole address. It would be a huge violation of my parole time if they found out I wasn't living there. My new parole officer was located in the Compton unit office. They do house visits to make sure the parolees are staying at the addresses given.

During my first week in L.A., I stayed a couple of nights with my sister where I should have always been staying. The following week, I had to see my parole officer for the first time. He was black and really cool. In fact, all the officers were black because it was Compton, California. I went into his office and reported in to him. He was telling me he wouldn't be hard on me and they did things different in L.A. He wanted me to report one time a month and on the second of every month. I said, "No problem, Sir!" He was looking in my file and said, "You used to play that ball, I see." "Yes sir, I was trying out for the Kings and I played in the summer pro league and in college." As he was looking and turning papers to see who was in front of him he said, "What's up with Stanford in your file? Your rap sheet is not that bad, just your first time in prison. Don't steal anything or take anything from anyone. I better not get any calls on you about threats or arrest or complaints and we will get along just fine, Sanders. Got it?" "Yes sir!" I said. He was cool and set up a house visit with me that following week. I knew when he was coming and he said he would let me off parole if I just did what he told me to do. I was blind to the fact I had my way with him so good. I started to use the system and break all my conditions of parole.

As time went on, I was hanging out with my two younger brothers, watching and noticing the things that they had. They were hustlers themselves. That following summer, I was in training camp with Magic Johnson's traveling team and the summer pro-league at the Long Beach Pyramid. Things were happening so fast when I moved down to L.A. It's almost as if I lost focus of my belief system and my faith. It seemed I was doing anything I could to play professional basketball since I was still young and talented. People saw me as a professional athlete because I was 6'7" and athletic-looking. I was using my sister's address as my own but I never really lived with her. Every time my parole officer would call or surprise visit her house, she would call me and tell me that my parole officer was there. My heart would always beat really fast because it would be a violation if he found out that I wasn't really living there. My brother-in-law, her husband, called me on my cell phone one day to tell me, "Hey man, your parole officer just left here, wanting to come in and do a house search. I told him no, and he wanted to know what room you stayed in." My brother-in-law told him I don't have a room and that I sleep on the couch. My brother-in-law tells me that this is crazy and he can't have this in his house. I kept telling him I would transfer my parole soon, but I never did because the parole officer kind of laid off coming over like that.

In the meantime, I was living in Corona, California, which is a forty-five-minute drive from my sister's house in Carson. The place I was renting was $1,800 a month. I started liking glamorous things like new cars and keeping the image of a professional ballplayer. I enjoyed using rental cars, especially the luxury ones. I had a beautiful blue 1995 BMW. The rental cars I liked were Lexus, BMW, and Mercedes-Benz. I recall my younger brother telling me how to make fast money with this check scam. I used to hang out at his apartment in Hawthorne and watch him clean his nice Jaguar and Benz in the back where everyone hung out. It's funny because he was living in low-income housing with really nice cars. I knew my brother was a hustler and a damn good one! He has done a little time as well. At the time, I think he was on federal parole. His Mercedes was dark black with tinted windows and you couldn't even see in it. It had nice rims with low-profile tires. I asked him, "Man, how are you doing it?" He said, "Man, I don't want to get you in no trouble, I know you're on parole." I replied, "You're on federal parole." "Ralph, you have the right persona, and carry yourself in a whole different manner than we do. You can make a killing by meeting girls in Hollywood, Westwood, Beverly Hills, Santa Monica, Brentwood, and nice areas like that. You are able to talk to anybody." I asked him to tell me how he's doing it. He said he had these company checks; all you have to do is fill them in and pass them to girls and have them cash them into their ATM machines. I asked him, "What do you mean?" I didn't completely understand what he was saying, but later on it dawned on me. My checks from the past that I did time for were quite different. It was small money and a lot of time. All I had to do back then was forge a signature and cash them myself. Well now this was a whole different ball game. He sold me two of them. The amount and name on the check were blank. My brother had all kinds of checks like that. He didn't steal them; rather other people gave them to him and he gave some to me.

At the time, I was working at Target in Corona by my house. It was a brand new Target and they were looking for team member managers. I was one of them and made over $14.00 an hour. What's interesting is that my parole officer never knew about my employment. The reason why is because I was working and living past the 50-mile radius of my parole. I didn't realize just how slick I had been until things started to catch up to me. One day I decided to quit my job because it was interfering with me trying to make time for basketball. So I put in my two weeks' notice. I really enjoyed working there. It paid my bills and I worked full time at 40 hours per week. I was only bringing in $1,500.00 a month, and still was short on cash to pay bills. I had a way with women, who did things for me like help pay my bills. I guess you could say that I was a player—not just a basketball player. I was taking my training really seriously and driving almost every other day to UCLA to train with the summer pro-league team. We had our first game at Long Beach Pyramid, where all the pro-athletes train for the summer in the league. I didn't do too well. I was on a really good team and didn't get too much playing time. There was a lot of talent in Los Angeles. What a great feeling to play with pro-athletes and train with them and try to fulfill my dream even though I was still on parole. It seems that my ex-wife left my heart. I didn't think much about her, maybe because I was living my life in the fast lane. Love for the world was making me feel apart from God. "IF ANY ONE LOVES THE WORLD, LOVE FOR THE FATHER IS NOT IN HIM" (1 John 2:15). In other words, you can't wholeheartedly love the world and God at the same time. Love for the world pushes out love for God, and love for God pushes out love for the world. "Delight yourself in the Lord and he will give you the Desires of your heart" (Psalms 37:4). With God's love we can delight in Him and desire for those things that are healthy for us and bring us life more abundantly. I didn't attend church any longer. It's almost as if I fell by the wayside like Jesus explains in the book of Mark: "Some seed fell on rocky ground where there wasn't much dirt. That seed grew very fast, because the ground was not deep. But when the sun rose, the plants dried up because they did not have deep roots. Some other seed fell among thorny weeds, which grew and choked the good plants. So those plants did not produce a crop. Some other seed fell on good ground and began to grow. It got taller and produced a crop. Some plants made thirty times more, some made sixty times more, and some made a hundred times more" (Mark 4:5-9).

I was the seed on rocky ground. I never realized that its tainted fruit determines a bad tree and its ripe fruit determines a good tree. It seemed I had everything on my tree that was both bad and good. I wish I could have realized back then that you can't serve God and this world. No one can serve two masters. Either he will hate the one and love the other, or he will be devoted to the one and despise the other. You cannot serve both God and Money (Matthew 6:24). My heart was basically running from God, and I started getting involved in something that was going to send me away for a very long time. Sometimes life takes you on adventures that you never thought would happen. Well, I had those checks and I held onto them for two weeks. I needed money. I didn't have my job any longer since I quit. I just spent a lot of time with basketball and the fast life. It seemed like the basketball was rolling me far away from my belief. This wasn't getting me anywhere and I never made any pro team, so I pretended to be something that I wasn't. I remember driving my nice car down Crenshaw Boulevard and Olympic. These girls were flirting with me. There were a couple of them in a car so I waved them over. We began to talk as I focused on the driver. All I had to do was pretend to be this professional basketball player to earn her trust and have her cash the check into her account. She said, "Nice car." I heard her other friends whisper to her friends that I was a basketball player. I took advantage of that whisper in my conversation with her. As we exchanged numbers, we were talking about each other's lives and what we did. She was a registered nurse and I was supposed to be a professional basketball player for the Utah Jazz and going to my home in the Wilshire District, a very prestigious neighborhood. I knew that would impress them and it did. I called her later that evening and took her to dinner. Of course, I paid for the dinner and the movie. I tried to make her think I was a "baller," which is like a high roller—someone with a lot of cash. One day we were on the Santa Monica pier, and as I was holding her hand and whispering down her neck and making her laugh, I mentioned to her, "You know what? Someone stole my wallet and I can't find it." She said, "Oh my God, are you serious? The wallet you had with you at dinner the other night?" She asked if I cancelled everything and I told her that I did and reported everything stolen. "My coach is giving me a $2,000.00 check to cash, but I can't cash it because I don't have any identification. I was wondering if maybe you could cash it for me since you have your ID." She said, "Sure, how can I cash it if it's written in your name?" "No, my coach left the name blank because he knew I was going to ask a friend to cash it for me." She nodded. "Oh, okay." We went to her ATM machine after walking on the pier. The check was in my pocket. I put her name on the check and she deposited it into her ATM machine. She gave me $300.00 out right away because that's all that was available at the time. Two days later, I asked her, "Can you please call and see if my check has cleared." She said it usually takes three working days. So I told her to check and see if it posted. She went to the ATM to check on her balance and $2,200.00 was available as of that day. (It was not cleared yet but posted as available.) The next morning, when the bank opened at 9, I brought her to the bank. As I sat in my car because I was afraid to go in with her, I sent her into the bank to make a $2,200.00 cash withdrawal. She walked back with this white envelope in her hand. As I saw her approaching the car, I was getting this happy feeling because I was getting paid. As she got in the car, she said, "Here you go. Are hundreds okay?" I said, "Sure." I put it in the glove compartment right in front of her knees and said, "Thank you, baby," and kissed her. At that moment, I wanted to drop her off and get rid of her, which I did. She thought my name was Chris Smith, a name I made up, and that I played professional basketball and lived somewhere that I didn't. To be honest, she knew nothing about me but what I looked like. I spent the $2,200.00 faster than I made it. I was getting more checks and finding more victims to cash them for me.

I remember meeting this girl in Beverly Hills, California. We were at the same stoplight and she flirted with me and I flirted with her. She drove a really nice Lexus. As the light turned green, she took off and made a right turn a couple of lights up. I decided to follow her because I saw her as a potential victim. She drove into a Radio Shack parking lot and got out of her car. I said to myself, "Wow, she's nice."

She looked like she came from a well-to-do family. She was wearing black high-heeled boots with leggings and a tight sweater. As I got out of the car and walked into Radio Shack, I had a plan. I acted as if I was there for the same reason, which was to buy something. I purposely bumped right into her.

She said, "You were driving the Black Lexus." I replied, "Yes, how are you? What a coincidence, what are you getting?" She said she was looking for wires to go from her speakers to her TV. I told her I know exactly what she needs because I just bought a really big screen TV and I think I know what you need. I offered to help her. I asked her where she was from and she said Beverly Hills. I told her I was from Palo Verdes, which is a very prestigious neighborhood. She asked me what I did for a living and if I played basketball. I told her, "Yes, I am trying out for the L.A. Lakers. I'm in camp this summer and they brought me over from Hamburg, Germany, because that's where I was playing semi-pro basketball." She seemed impressed by what I was telling her. I was winning her over so fast and knew this would take no time. I asked her about going to dinner later tonight. She responded, "Yes, I have never been out with a pro-basketball player. How long have you been playing?" I told her all my life. She thought it was very cool. So I picked her up for dinner around 7. We went to a really nice place in Santa Monica. It's interesting because I really liked this girl. I was attracted to many of my victims because they were beautiful women. It seemed I attracted a majority of women that were very independent, well off, and somewhat gullible—or should I say I was just really manipulative. When I picked her up she allowed me to come inside on the second floor of some condominiums in the Wilshire District of Los Angeles. This girl had a great smile and seemed very faithful. We decided to go to dinner in Santa Monica and had a great time. We had a couple of cocktails as we laughed and talked about who we were and what we did. Of course, I lied about everything I said and did. It was almost as if it was natural for me to tell lies and to impress her. I made sure she watched me as I pulled out my wallet, which was a big, black wallet with all my credit cards lined up and a sum of cash in it. She must have thought in her mind that I was a very organized and wealthy man. The night ended so I dropped her off and kissed her goodnight and headed home thinking this would be easy. The Bible tells us, "AS A MAN THINKETH, SO IS HE" (Proverbs 23:7). Human action begins from our innermost thoughts.

As I drove home to Corona around 11:30 p.m., I was thinking about what I was really doing. I just couldn't seem to come to my senses that what I was doing was wrong. There were times when I really wanted to stop. This girl was just one of the few that I'd victimized so far. I thought to myself, I am breaking all my parole conditions and living a secret life. I was pretty good at it. So good that I started fooling myself into thinking I was the person I was portraying myself to be. Well the morning came and first thing at 9:00 a.m. I called her and told her this big story. "You won't believe what happened last night when I left your house. I stopped at a 7-11 off of Wilshire Blvd. and I left my top down. There was a homeless person outside who was begging for money before I went in. I gave him $10.00 as I was sitting in my car. Not thinking, I left my wallet sitting there on my seat while I was inside the store using the restroom. I realized when I got home that I didn't have my wallet and thought I lost it. But I think the homeless person from 7-11 stole it while I was in the restroom." She said, "Oh my God, did you cancel all your credit cards?" I said, "Yes, I just did before I called you. I cancelled my American Express, my MasterCard, Visa, and even my Mervyn's and J.C. Penny's cards. I called the bank and they told me they are going to put a hold on my account for five business days because they were investigating everything." She said, "Is there anything I can do to help?" I thought,

Perfect timing! My chance to give her a check. I told her that my coach left me a check for $5,000.00, but since I lost my ID he left the name blank so I could have one of my friends or families cash it. "I guess I can help you cash it." I told her, "No, I don't know you that well. I don't want you to be responsible for all that money in your account. But I guess I can deposit it in your account and let it sit there for a couple of days rather than carrying it around." She said, "You can trust me, it's safe. I'll even give you my account and pin number." "I will pick you up for brunch, there's a really nice restaurant I want to take you to in Beverly Hills." "What time?" "How about 10:30 sharp?" "I will see you soon." I called my brother immediately and bragged about the situation, telling him I got one as though I caught a fish or a guppy.

As I headed over to pick her up, she got in the car; she seemed so sad that I had my wallet ripped off. She asked me if I would like to deposit the check now. I said, "Sure." As we parked in front of the bank at the ATM machine, I told her how beautiful she looks and how good she smells. I guess it's like putting icing on the cake before you eat it. So I wrote the check in her full name and she deposited it in the ATM machine. She immediately gave me $300.00 that she could withdraw and gave me the remaining balance in two days. Once I received that, I disappeared out of her life, leaving her empty-handed and without a clue as to my identity. Like I mentioned earlier, I stayed in luxury rental cars and gave false names and pretended to be this pro-athlete. That following week, I was driving to practice at UCLA to practice with Magic Johnson's traveling team. I thought to myself, I need to stop doing what I'm doing, but something kept telling me to keep doing it.

That same day, around 1:00 p.m. after playing ball, I met this girl and this guy in Westwood. She flirted with me first and, of course, I took advantage of it and told her I was a junior at USC and on the basketball team. I gave her an alias name. I said, "Hi, my name is Derek." She said her name was Amy. I said, "Is that your boyfriend, the guy that just walked into the bookstore?" She said, "No, I'm single." I said, "Oh, okay, what are you studying at UCLA?" She replied, "History." I asked her if she liked it; she said that she did and asked what I was majoring in, "Basketball?" She was being sarcastic because I was tall and athletic-looking. I said, "P.E. (Physical Education) is my major but hopefully I will get into the pros." She said, "Oh, I think we play USC next Thursday." I said, "Oh, that's right we do. So let's hang out tonight." We went to a movie but I can't remember what we saw. She met me there. The next day we went to the mall and hung out and did a little shopping. I bought her a pair of tennis shoes and a shirt. I tried to make her think that I was a nice guy and that I had money and came from a good family. I convinced her to cash a check as well. I told her I needed a favor because I misplaced my ID and couldn't find it. I told her I thought I had left it at a club a couple of nights ago and that I really needed her to cash this $2,000.00 check. "Do you think I can trust you with my money if I put it in your account?" She said, "Come on, are you kidding me? Your money is safe with me." "Okay, I just need to know how to spell your name so my coach will know what name to put it in. I will call him right now." As I was on the phone, I thought to myself, acting as if I were talking to my coach in front of her, making her think he was on the phone, when in actuality I never dialed anybody. I said, "See you tomorrow at practice, Coach," and hung up the phone. I told her it was cool and that my coach would give me a check in the morning. "Are you sure I can trust you? I just met you two days ago. She said, "Come on, you know my full name and what school I go to. You can trust me." "Okay, I'll get the check tomorrow. I have to go and pick up my brother now. Let's meet for lunch tomorrow." She said she couldn't because she had a psychology class at 12:30 p.m. "How about 2:00 p.m.?" I asked. She said that would be fine. I told her I would pick her up in front of Fat Burgers in Westwood. So the next day, I picked her up and told her, "I'm sorry, I only have 30 minutes, our coach called a basketball practice. Maybe we should go to dinner tonight." We deposited a check for $2,000.00 and it cleared in two days. My intention was to get what I wanted and move on. I was so selfish and didn't realize that one day all of this would come back on me.

Every time I left my victim, I had a sense of guilt but it never lasted. The guilt seemed to vanish after I had the money in my hands. As time went on, I was only paroled in L.A. for 10 months at this point and had no idea I was being investigated.

7

Fox News – L.A.'s Most Wanted

One morning I was at Bally's Gym in Corona, California, working out and having a good morning. Everyone there thought I was this big-shot ball player. I always kept a fake alias. It was almost as if it was my safety net because I was on parole breaking all of my conditions. My intentions were never to hurt anyone physically or mentally. I just thought I was doing what was natural to survive. However I was Hustlin' others; I was Half-timin' and lyin'. My basketball situation seemed to go nowhere and I continued to still find victims and do what I was best at. I got a call from one of the personal trainers at the gym and he told me, "I think some detectives are looking for you." I freaked out and said, "Me?" They showed a picture of you and asked if we had seen you working out. I told him that you work out here but didn't know where you live. I told them your name. They said it wasn't your name. I said, "Okay, dude, and thanks," and hung up. I remember him telling me on the phone that I wasn't in trouble, that they just wanted to ask me some questions. The trainer asked me where I was going on and if everything was all right. I said, "Yeah, I am. It's probably my ex-wife looking for me to sign some documents." I was really nervous and the first thing I did was call my sister (where my parole was) on the phone. She was yelling at me over the phone saying that she'd been trying to reach me for two hours. She explained there were five cop cars, a helicopter, and two parole officers with vests banging on my screen door. "Bam, Bam, Bam...Parole Search! Where's Ralph Sanders? We know he doesn't live here." My sister said, "He doesn't." At that time, I knew I was in trouble. Wow, where do I go from here? I was scared to go out my front door. I guess my sister and brother-in-law didn't tell where I lived, they just said I didn't live there. They were tired of all the drama I was bringing to the house. So they pretty much told the truth. I didn't realize any of these things until I was in custody. I was getting a U-Haul truck that same day. My mind was moving really fast. I had a girl staying with me from Cameron Park. She had moved down to L.A. with me. I had her so deceived that she would do anything for me. She freaked out about this situation when she came home from working at the Tyler Mall in Riverside, California. She was in sales and worked at a clothing store called J.J. Riggins. This relationship was such a short period of time. But I shared this to show just how caught up I was in money, lusts, and lies. I know this adds insult to injury. Well, today was the day I had to make a move. I didn't have any sad feelings because my blood pressure was moving so fast because of what my sister told me over the phone. She was really upset, and all I could think in my mind was that my parole officer was looking for me. I immediately with no doubt put all my stuff in storage. My neighbors were asking questions. "Hey, Sanders! Where you going?" I tell them I have an emergency. I am going to Europe

to play basketball. My agent got me a job there. My neighbors were always concerned about everyone else's business. Did I fail to mention that this was the day before the O. J. Simpson verdict? Everybody was outside in our neighborhood talking about the verdict. And the next day, I was moving out of my house. I was too scared to report to my parole officer or even call him. So I had my girlfriend call the parole office on her cell phone and ask them if they had seen Ralph Sanders because she was looking for him. She didn't give them her name. They asked her why she was concerned. She said, "I was calling to see if I could find him. I am looking for him. He's a friend of mine." The parole officer told her that if she sees him to tell him he's in a lot of trouble. I whispered and told her to hang up. My conscience just wanted to know what was going on even though I knew exactly what was happening. I just needed to talk to my sister to get clarification from her; however, we were not talking because we were not that "tight" (close).

Did I fail to mention that while all of this was going on I also had a girlfriend? Well, my girlfriend (at the time) and I had a fight and she took off to Northern California with everything she could in the back of her car. That was the end of that story and the short relationship. I used her too. The first three days I camped out at my brother's house and didn't realize I was absconding, which means running, on parole. Absconding is a one-year violation flat. That wouldn't make any difference compared to the time I might be facing.

That following night, my younger brother, who goes by the name Lorenzo, was running a nightclub as a DJ, and some of my family members were there at a place called Geraldine's off of Crenshaw and Imperial. It was around 8:30 p.m. I drove by. We were all just partying and drinking and visiting one another. I remember I was wearing a green Nike sweat suit and green Kenny Griffin basketball shoes—like the Boston Celtics colors. I tried to look the part of a ball player. I remember this because I was in the mall a couple of days earlier and met these two Swedish girls. I was supposed to meet one of them that night around 9:30 p.m. at the Doubletree Hotel off of Century Boulevard, right down the street from LAX. So I thought I would kill some time visiting my brother and some other family members that were there. Everything was moving so fast for me. I stayed in hotel rooms after I moved my stuff into storage and moved from place to place. After leaving Geraldine's and saying good-bye to my brother, I drove 15 minutes away to the hotel to meet my date. As I was driving down Century Boulevard, I looked to my right at the Hilton, which was around the corner from my hotel, and there was a gathering of a lot of people in the valet parking. I was always looking for potential victims. I valet parked my car and got out. Immediately, the two valets treated me as if I had a room there. I walked into the lobby and told the valets to park my car right out front as I would only be about 10 minutes. As I was walking in, people were staring at me and some people wanted my autograph. It seemed that once two people looked at me, everyone looked at me. I walked into the lobby and sat down in the bar area. There was a huge screen TV that covered one side of the wall. There were a lot of girls and guys dressed nicely and they were just staring at me. I talked to this one beautiful girl and said, "Hey, sweetie. What's your name?" She told me her name and said she was only spending one night there because she was a stewardess. She stared me down and said, "Which one are you?" I said, "I'm Sean Anderson from the Boston Celtics." She said, "I thought so." This was just a made-up name. There was no Sean Anderson of the Boston Celtics. She gave me her phone number because I was in a hurry. She said she would be back in Los Angeles the following week and we could set up a date. I told her that would be great because I was there for the summer pro league, and what was so funny about this is that I really was in the summer pro league.

I got my car from the valet and tipped the guys $20.00 and drove to the Doubletree just around the corner, not realizing I was just aired on television on Fox News' *L.A.'s Most Wanted*. I didn't know this at the time. I learned this from my family later. They had a picture of me with my green sweat suit and green shoes leaving the Hilton Hotel. As I drove up into the Doubletree parking lot, the valet knew exactly who I was—Chris Smith, a Clippers' player that had checked in the day before. They looked up to me, and one of the valets asked if he could have a picture and autograph. I was happy to do that for him. I had a way of pleasing others, and I guess you could say, pleasing myself. As I walked into the lobby, two of the valets asked if I had a good dinner and proceeded to tell me that there was a beautiful tall woman with an accent waiting for me in the lobby. As I walked past the concierge, they all greeted me and asked about my day. They also told me about the woman waiting for me. I turned around to tell the valet to leave my car up front because I was going to take my date somewhere else. As I approached her she looked stunning, wearing a long black coat and high heels. I really wanted to sleep with this girl and have a little fun before I gave her a check. In my car, I had a check all ready. I just wanted to spend time with her and get to know her for some reason. As I approached her and hugged her, she smelled really good and seemed happy to see me. We walked to the front toward the doors to go to the valet. We were indecisive about what we were going to do. Neither of us was hungry. I told her I had that check I was talking about a couple of days ago. She said, "Okay, the one from your coach?" I told her, "Yes, we can deposit it later at the ATM. But let's go to the beach now, I have a blanket in the back of my car." She liked that idea. Come to think of it, my curiosity was wondering if she was even wearing anything under that coat! She was somewhat gullible and excited to be with me.

We walked to the car and a lady and a man walked right up to us before we walked out of the hotel and asked if they could take a picture of me and my "wife." We all got in the picture and the man told me I had a great season. He told me he was always a Celtics fan. The valet pulled my car up and saw me walk through the double doors looking like cash with my green sweat suit and green shoes and my beautiful date. They opened the car doors for us, she got in first, I was about to tip the valet, and before I could even bend my head down to get in the car, I looked up and saw a helicopter with lights beaming down into the parking lot. Several police cars with sirens passed by and eight or nine cars pulled up. One pointed a gun at my head and said, "Hey you! Don't get in the car! Step away from the car right now!" I said, "What's going on, Officer?" He said, "Just do as I say, right now! Right now!" I stepped away from the car and immediately two cops approached me from the back of my car and politely put me in handcuffs. It seemed to me that they really didn't know who I was, but I learned later they likely had a report of me being in the vicinity of the hotel that Fox News had just aired on TV. As the other cops told my date to get out of the car, they started asking her questions about how she met me. A couple minutes later, I came up as the suspect they were looking for. They put me in a prone position on the concrete on the valet parking floor. They handcuffed me and treated me aggressively. I was shoved into the back of the police car. As I mumbled to the officer, "What's going on?" he said, "You will find out later." I was in such a state of shock that I don't even remember being read my Miranda rights, but I know they did. As I was looking out the window of the police car, everyone was staring at me—the concierge, the valets, the hotel guests, and the couple who had just taken a photo with us. Fox News drove up in their van to get the story. My date started crying as she was staring at me. The cops were telling her about me and who I was. She was going to be my next victim. I started thinking in my heart that this was all wrong and it's just a dream that will end tomorrow. I will wake up and this would never have happened. The cops asked me as we were driving to the county jail, "Mr. Sanders, why didn't you run?" I said, "Run from what?" They laughed at me. I told them, "I just want to talk to my attorney. I don't want to talk." One cop said, "Well, I'm sure this isn't your first rodeo. So it shall be."

8

L.A. County Blues

April 1996

As we got to the glasshouse at the L.A. County Jail, they put me in this huge holding tank that was really filthy, smelly, and oddly there were homeless people lying on the floor. There were about 15 people in the holding tank. There was one phone on the wall that could be used to call collect. I called my sister and there was a block on the phone, meaning she wouldn't accept collect calls. I guess it was the same block that was there when I was in San Quentin. So I called my brother and he accepted my call. He said, "Man, I just saw you on TV. They got you, huh?" I didn't cry and acted as if I wasn't guilty. I was always the type of person who wouldn't cry in front of other people. There were 15 bodies surrounding me in the tank—some asleep and some awake. I just held in my tears. I told my brother I needed an attorney, and the detectives came in so I had to hang up because they wanted to talk to me. One detective, a black lady, sat me down in a chair at her desk and said, "Mr. Sanders, your mother is on the phone. Do you want to talk to her?" I said that I did and she said, "I will give you a moment with her." I got on the phone. "Mama?" She said, "Boy, what have you done? I knew you was doin' that." I said, "Mama, watch these phones, they are recording." I was thinking to myself that my mother and I weren't really "tight" (close). I would pay her rent at times and we'd see each other once in a while, but not much. I remember her visiting my house in Corona that previous summer to swim and hang out with my other brothers. This was going through my conscience as I was talking to her, and tears started rolling down my eyes. I couldn't hold my emotions any longer. My mother said, "It's okay, baby. Hold on. Your brothers will try to get you an attorney. The detective lady said you are fighting three strikes." I asked her, "What's that, Mama?" She said, "You can get 25 years to life." I said, "What?" I told her that it didn't make sense. She said, "I guess they are putting the charges on you now." I said, "Mama, I have got to go. I love you. They have to house me." I started talking to the detective lady. She was taking my gold chain and Rolex watch off my wrist. She also took my wallet and put it with my property. She asked if I wanted my mother to come in and pick it up. I said yes. Anyway, there I was, about to face the big house—L.A. County blues. They line us all up and walk us through some doors and call us by name and tell us to strip down. These sheriffs were different. They were so aggressive that I actually saw them beat other inmates down. I mean really beat them up, and we could not turn our heads around. This place was infested with gang members everywhere. I didn't fit the environment but my crimes did. At the time I didn't realize but I belonged there just as much as those gang members. Little did I know that I would be spending the next eight months of my life there.

They started to house us and strip us down and put us in blues...L.A. County blues. They gave us towels rolled up with underwear, socks, and powdered toothpaste. I knew that I was back in jail and that I might not be getting out. The parole violation was going through my conscious along with everything else. We had to see somebody one by one to place us in a housing unit. They put a red band around my wrist and separated me and another inmate from the other eight. They sent us to a totally different place than the county jail. This place was huge and had escalators. Can you imagine a jail with escalators? It looked like a mall without the stores. They housed me with a bunch of other inmates in barracks and shut me in. As I looked forward I saw nothing but bunk beds with over 100 inmates. Now I was locked inside with them. Everyone stopped and looked at me. I was walking down the aisle of this huge room with people gambling in the corner, some people were doing drugs, homosexuals in one corner, blacks and whites separated, Hispanics had their own area. It was almost as if I was in a detention center with a capacity of 150 men. Everyone had his or her own bunk. As I walked toward the back, a brother approached me and shook my hand and said, "Hey, brother man—you on the bottom. I like the top." As I set up my stuff, which wasn't very much, just my bedding, I wanted a phone call. I looked toward the walls and there were six phones, but none of them were working! I was told there's a switch that the officers use to turn the phones on and off depending on the behavior of the inmates. I asked my bunkie, "What happened to the phones? They don't work." He said, "The phones are off for three weeks. We had a riot in here three weeks ago and they separated a lot of the inmates into other pods." The inmates were separated to keep tension down between the races, mainly blacks and whites. I didn't understand any of this stuff, but started to vaguely remember because I had been to prison before. This wasn't my first "rodeo." Sad to say but I was kind of hip to the system. L.A. County Jail was a different story. Here, there were a lot of gang members and stuff I didn't understand too well. But there is one thing I do understand—the politics of surviving in here. They told us to get in our bunks as I heard this loudspeaker: "Chow release in ten minutes!"

Two sheriffs walked in the door. "Everyone off their bunks! Line up for chow! Get in the order that your bunk is in and follow the person in front of you. There will be no talking." I thought to myself, this is new. They do things different here in the county jail than they do in San Quentin. Walking in blue amongst all the rules. I had to put on my game face because many of the guys in here looked pretty rough. I guess we all had a game face. I am not speaking of a basketball game face. It was more like a "don't talk to me" game face. As I went through the chow line, I noticed inmates were serving food. They called them trustees, meaning they had a different color prison uniform (in khaki). These inmates served food. They were serving time in the L.A. County Jail doing a task; culinary arts was their work. I couldn't believe what I saw on my plate, the nasty gravy and meat they call "shit on the shangle."

I saw my little brother as he looked me in the eye to give me my serving. He said, "Man, whatcha doin' in here?" I said, "I got caught, man, and I heard I was on TV." My brother said, "What? Hey, I'm gonna try to slip you some extra food later because we're about to clean up—you're the last building, give me three minutes. I will slide you some powdered eggs and sausage." "I love you, man." "Cool, I love you, too." I thought to myself when I sat down at the table with four other inmates, No one talks to no one because we only have six minutes to eat. I started thinking I forgot my brother was in the county doing seven months for identity fraud. It felt weird seeing him here because I was worried about his protection. He's not as big and tall as myself, but he's from the hood and he knows the gangs. I think he's part of the Crips. He never had time to slip me the extra food, but I was okay because I didn't like the stuff anyway. I couldn't eat it. I was too used to fancy high-class restaurants. As we got up and were escorted back into our module, "Classification" wanted to see me. I asked my bunkie what it was for and he told me they were going to be housing me into another cell on the other side of the jail. I asked,

"Why do I have to go to a cell?" He said, "Brother man, I don't know what you done but have you looked at your wrist lately? You fighting three strikes!" As I looked at my wrist, I didn't really pay attention to the number 3. I thought it meant module 3 or section 3. I remembered in classification, they told me I was fighting 25 to life and they were housing me with other three-strikers. I was with some crazy people—I mean people that didn't give a damn. They put me on the third tier and I had my own cell. It's kind of funny because all of the cells were always open. We had a TV that the guards would push out for us to watch. It was this really old TV that looked like it was from the '50s. It was like our own little world. Some people were fighting 175 years and other inmates were fighting their first case, which was a murder, or manslaughter, or rape, or repeat offenders such as myself fighting the three strikes.

I couldn't wait to go to court the following Tuesday and find out what was really going on with my case. I finally got to use the phone because we had one on our tier. We could only call collect and I called my older brother. He accepted my call and told me don't take any deals. Those burglaries from your past are not real strikes. I didn't understand what he was talking about and we only had 10 minutes to talk. The phone kept beeping every 10 seconds throughout my conversation. It was very irritating and we couldn't discuss anything. My brother kept promising that he would be in court and raise funds for an attorney but it never happened. I needed $10,000.00 for a retainer for an attorney to handle a three-strikes case. My family didn't have that kind of money. If they did, I wouldn't have been doing these things in the first place. I was all on my own just like in San Quentin. But there's one thing I had back then—a wife and conjugal visits. However, this time around I had no one because my girlfriend had left me. Fortunately for myself I did have other girls coming to visit me here in the county jail. There were girls that I didn't give checks to, girlfriends. One of the sheriffs that runs our module pulled me aside during lunchtime and said, "Hey you, Sanders, come here," with his partner next him. They said, "Hey, ain't you the guy that was on TV a week ago for posing as a professional basketball player and passing bad checks?" I said, "Yes, sir, that was me." "What was your motive, Sanders?" "I can't talk about my case with anyone." "Hey, did you sleep with a lot of those girls? Were they really fine? Did you really play pro ball?" I told them, "Yes, I did. I played semi-pro ball." The sheriffs thought this was pretty cool because I didn't fit the criteria of other inmates. They were wondering why I was wearing the red band. I didn't seem like the type of guy that did prison time before so the band threw them off. On the way back from lunch, they pulled me out of line again. Some of the other inmates were getting suspicious because they thought maybe I was snitching. This is something you don't do in L.A. County Jail is talk too long with the sheriffs. They gave me a job being a "khaki trustee" in the third-strike module. In this situation I was...getting special privileges because of my appearance and demeanor.

It was 2:15 p.m. and they called me in for a visit over the loudspeaker. Here I am, four months in the county jail, and strangely I am called for a visit. Two of the guys in the cell next to me said, "Hey bro, you got a visit!...One of your girls? You go, player!"

Having a visit was a really big thing. It showed a support system; some inmates get jealous of this. As I was escorted for my visit to the visiting room, it was an ugly sight. There were tall windows separating the inmates from the visitors about 40 booths long. Some inmates were crying, some were loud, some were happy, and some were scared. And myself, I was just curious as to who was there to visit me. I knew it wasn't my girlfriend that lived with me. As I sat in the booth, there she was, the girl from Stockton. I only knew her for four weeks and somehow she found me there. As I put my hand up to the glass window to touch her hand—she was with another friend—the first thing she told me was "Don't cry." I let my emotions come out at that moment. She said she had to tell me something. She said she was four-months pregnant. I didn't know how to react to this because of all my emotions that revolved around my current situation. I wanted her to have the baby and stick with me through all this time. That would be insane for her to do, but it would be a sense of security for me. I told myself if I have to do a lot of time, at least I will have a family. Apparently, it didn't happen. I received a letter from her a week later from one of her friends stating that she was in the hospital. She had gotten into a car accident on the way back to Sacramento.

The steering wheel had pushed into her stomach and she lost the baby. When I read the letter, I didn't have any strong feelings about it because I didn't really know her that well. My feelings were still elsewhere. I never heard from her again.

As time went by, I began programming and feeling my way around the system. We were let out for recess by each unit and I came across my other younger brother. That is three of six children in jail. Either we were Hustlin' too much or the justice system was very biased. But the fact is we were there. This now made two of my brothers I saw in there. He was there for outstanding tickets he didn't pay. I really helped him out because I had a lot of privilege in the jail after being there for almost six months. I got my brother moved up to my module to be in the cell with me. But since they found out he wasn't a three-striker, they moved him out. He was going home anyway in a couple of weeks. That was the last I saw of my brothers for a long time. I started reading the Bible again and praying when I was alone. I guess I did it out of boredom, but later I began reading it out of true faith. Something started to happen to me as time went on. There were these two guys on my tier. One they called Big Mike. He was a big guy—6'7", weighing at least 250 pounds. The other guy was short, light-skinned, sneaky, and conniving. He was fighting 25 to life. We were all trustees, and in the beginning these guys tried to pull a crazy stunt on me to get me into trouble so I would lose my special privileges with the officers; they were a little jealous.

One day, the sergeant and three sheriffs pulled me into their office and asked me, "What is this, Sanders?" I had no idea what they were pulling me in for. I thought maybe I had a call from home that someone had died or was hurt. The sergeant reached into his drawer and pulled out a shank about a foot long with a lot of tape around it to hold it together. It had the unit deputy names written on it. The sergeant deputy said this was found on my bunk. I was in a state of shock. I told them I had no idea why I was being accused of having this. He said, "Sanders, we know this is not your character. You're a con man, not a violent person. I don't know why you are wearing the three-strike band, but the court system does what it does and we are here to supervise all of you. So I advised my deputies not to send you back to your tier because you're in danger. Too much fraternizing with staff has gotten you into this so we are going to move you for your own safety." I told them, "Okay, thank you." Thank God. God is my judge.

During the eight months I spent at the L.A. County Jail, I was appointed a public defender. He and I never got along and it seemed that we couldn't agree on anything. He rarely visited me to talk with me about my case, nor did he provide me with the relevant information regarding the status of my charges. My intuition told me that it wasn't the nature of my crimes that angered him, rather it was the fact that my victims were all women. When we spoke, he appeared to never truly listen to what I had to say. He treated me as though I didn't have any rights. I knew that what I did was wrong and against the law, but I also knew that my crimes weren't violent. No physical harm was ever caused to anyone. But he treated me like a criminal. He always rushed through our meetings and never ever called me by name. Instead, he addressed me as "Guy." He would say, "Guy, you don't stand a chance so knock it off. Guy, you just need to take this deal." This man was supposed to be defending me, but he had no respect for me whatsoever.

When we would meet on rare occasions, it would be in what is known as "the cage." The cage is a cement room about the size of a bedroom—and not a master bedroom either. This place was small and it was overflowing with inmates. Everyone could hear what was being said. Nothing was private. My cellmates would tell me, "You need to fire that dump truck. He is not looking after you." How can that "guy" be my public defender?

My trip to the courthouse majorly affected who I am today. One afternoon on a bright sunny day, I remember seeing a clear blue sky. The skyscrapers of L.A. made a major impression on me and struck me as a beautiful sight. As is typical for Los Angeles, there were lots of cars on the freeways as people were driving to work and going about their daily business. Thoughts began running through my mind: "How did I let this happen? Why did I get myself into this predicament?" And then out of nowhere, a song by Etta James began playing. "Oh Happy Day" filled the silence of the bus. "When Jesus washed, when Jesus washed...He washed my sins away. Oh Happy Day!" These words filled my heart and soul and gave me hope in a situation that seemed impossible. I felt as though God himself was speaking to me through this song and reassuring me that I would be okay and would come through this triumphant with His help. I felt a sense of renewal and that this was a new beginning. This was a turning point in my journey.

I began to cry and knew that even though I was suffering, this pain was only temporary. This too shall pass, I thought. I got myself into this situation through sinning and turning away from God. At that point I knew I wanted my freedom again and there was only one way to get it: by refusing to go back to the old way of life that brought me here.

After arriving at the courthouse, I knew what I had to do. It was time to let my public defender go. "Line 15, The People versus Ralph Sanders." I stood up and immediately stated to the judge, "Your Honor, I want to fire my public defender." The judge inquired, "Why, Mr. Sanders?" I responded, "We do not see eye to eye and we constantly argue." The judge never made eye contact with me but looked down at my file before him and said, "Your appointed public defender is an excellent choice to handle your case. In my opinion, it would be foolish of you to let him go." So there I was, still stuck with my lousy public defender. I was angry and frustrated at the whole process. I was at a complete and total loss.

At my next court appearance, I decided to take the advice of my fellow inmates and "fire that dump truck" of a public defender. That's exactly what I did. The court held what is known as a Marsden hearing. This is a hearing that must be held when an attorney is court-appointed and the defendant requests a new lawyer. I informed the judge this time that I wanted to represent myself. In legal terms, this is called "in propia persona" or "in pro per," which means to act on one's own behalf. I was now representing myself and would be fighting the case against myself. I thought, Hey, at least I have a good relationship with myself. So on this new and happy day I received what I asked for. I could sense the judge didn't like my decision, but it was within my right to get rid of a public defender who wasn't after my best interest.

**Included in these next five pages is
the transcript from my Marsden hearing
held on October 16, 1996.**

Unfortunately, by representing myself, I didn't have a clue what to do. The judge reassigned the same public defender to my case. Once again, the conflict between us continued. We were back in court again and he advised that I should accept the plea bargain. This plea bargain was for a fifteen-year sentence in lieu of receiving 350 years or life. (I know you're probably laughing or in shock right now.) In hearing this, my heart was enraged, and I became fearful and lacked any trust in him. I was losing hope. And then I remembered, my fellow inmates told me I should fake a heart attack! And so I did. At that moment, I was completely desperate. I fell down and my body began to shake uncontrollably. I was drooling and I peed on myself while shaking. I remember someone asking if I was taking any seizure medication as I rolled my eyes up into their sockets. It worked...paramedics were called and I was given oxygen and taken to the hospital at U.S.C. (University of Southern California). I spent three days there and didn't have to eat a single peanut-butter sandwich. I was in a nice, comfy bed where a policeman guarded my door. I had temporarily escaped the confines of the L.A. County Jail.

The hospital cleared me for release and I found myself back in court. My heart attack/seizure stunt was merely a delay tactic because it was time to select a jury of 12. I tried to avoid the process because I feared the outcome. Previously, I had tried to retain an attorney I knew named Ron Ask. When I walked into the courtroom, I saw him. I was dropping tears at this point and I couldn't hold my head up high. I remember Ron rubbing my shoulder and whispering in my ear that I should take the deal. I couldn't believe my eyes that he was there. No one I knew was there. Not a friend and not even a family member. I was an emotional wreck at this point. My nose was dripping with mucus and I felt completely and utterly helpless. I thought I would die.

My attorney, Ronald Ask, wrote the following letter when he learned I was writing this story about my life. I thank him for this invaluable contribution to my story:

ELDER LAW CENTER, P.C.
Ronald W. Ask, Esq.

When I got to the courthouse, the jury had been picked, and they were all milling around out in the hallway. All the witnesses were there, probably about half a dozen to a dozen of them, and they were ready to start the trial. They held up the commencement of the trial until I got there. I had had a court appearance earlier in the morning, and I was probably 1/2 hour to an hour late. I was introduced around to the judge, and the prosecuting attorney. Ralph was in some dirty looking dungarees, handcuffed, and chained. The judge said, "Mr. Ask, I will give 5 minutes." I immediately started talking to Ralph. I explained to him that no matter what he thought, no matter how inconsequential the crime might have been that he was accused of committing, that he was going to spend the rest of his life in prison if he didn't listen to me. There were no ifs, ands or buts about it. The judge was offering to strike one of his strikes. That is to say that he would reduce him from a two-striker down to a one-striker, if he would plead guilty to these crimes, and then he would add another strike back on. So, instead of being a three-striker and you are out, he would be a two-striker and he would be sentenced to 15 years. He would actually serve 85%. Ralph just couldn't believe he was going to spend the next 12.75 years in prison.

Ralph was a really good-looking guy, 26 years old, college educated. He had never committed an act of violence in his life, but did do some dishonest things in his life. After about 4 minutes, the judge didn't even send the bailiff out to ask me how I was doing. He just walked out from his chambers and proceeded to take the bench. I screamed at Ralph. I said, "Ralph, you've got to take the deal. You can't think about this anymore." Finally, big tears began to flow out of his eyes, and down his cheeks. He said, "Mr. Ask, what do I have to do?" I said, "Just yell out to the court, 'Guilty. I plead guilty.'" So, he did. With about 2 or 3 seconds remaining, he said, "I plead guilty." With that, they proceeded with the sentencing. It was put right on the record that he was looking at 360 years. He had been charged and would have been found guilty, and there was no defense to his case, since they had all the evidence they needed.

A few minutes later, Ralph was whisked off, straight to San Quentin. The judge, along with the prosecuting attorney, and the public defender, and I found ourselves in the elevator together going downstairs for lunch. "Another day, another dollar. Another human being sentenced to 15 years... All in a day's work."

Without exaggeration, this was one of the most dramatic moments that I have ever had in my entire legal career, and I wasn't even the attorney representing him. Fast-forward to today, Ralph did 11 years, or 10 years and 11 months, and was stabbed, beaten, abused and finally took refuge in the chapel of the prison. He became a "Born Again Christian" and a good one.... To see how far this young man has come from what he went through, is a miracle. I just wanted to share this with you.

Sincerely, R.

9

Pleasant Valley State Prison

I was now on the Grey Goose Department of Corrections bus (the second time in my life) headed to Pleasant Valley State Prison located in Central California about 10 miles off of Highway 5. There was nothing on the highway—no gas stations, no hotels, and no restaurants. I spent a lot of hours on this bus staring out the tinted windows wondering how I was going to do all this time. I wasn't aware of anything, my emotional or my physical state, because I was in a state of shock. My mind was racing with thoughts about my girlfriend and all the girls I'd lied to and scammed. I thought to myself, *They were manipulated by me. They were manipulated by someone they trusted.* How awful they must have felt having been lied to. I was chained to another inmate in silence. There we were headed to the same world called punishment and suffering. As we drove up, the buildings looked so new and there were inmates out front working on the Pleasant Valley sign. I thought to myself this place is still in the process of construction. All of us on the bus could not believe how huge the prison was, without nothing surrounding it but dirt. As we approached it from a high hill from Highway 5, it reminded me of the Pentagon that I had seen on TV during 9/11. As we approached R&R, Receiving and Release, I learned fast that each yard had five buildings with the capacity to hold 500 inmates in each building. People are housed according to their classification points, meaning level of custody and minimum to maximum security. I started out in maximum security due to my sentencing. I was told that as an inmate serves time, points decrease and privileges increase.

I was put in a cell in Yard B with a black guy from San Diego that was part of a gang. I learned that he had already put in 15 years of his life sentence. I went through two gates and entered a huge day room with no bars but padded cells instead. I asked, "Why?" and was told by an officer that I was housed in Close Custody B. Close Custody B was a building that enabled the officers to observe me for five to eight. During this time I was restricted from going out at night into the yard like other inmates in the other buildings until classification could make a determination of my behavior and responses. Prisoners like myself, sentenced to serve this much time, needed to be watched to see if we could handle the thought of it or not. They knew it might cause us to become angered, commit suicide, or even hurt someone else badly out of frustration. All those with ten or more years of time go to this building. After an assessment is made, we are assigned to a lower custody building or stay in the same building. As I walked through that second gate, I was told to go upstairs to the last cell on the right and that the correction officer would unlock the door electronically. He was on a catwalk and could see everything happening below him, including the tunnel that connects the two gates in order to enter the day room. The day room had television, games, haircuts, and activities six hours daily.

From 9:00 a.m. to 9:00 p.m., every two hours, there was access to the yard as well as recreational activities such as weights, basketball, handball, and such. In the recreation yard inmates were separated by unwritten rules for territory. The "baddest" persons with a serious record of stabbings, life sentence, and so on are known as "shot callers." Blacks hung with blacks. Whites hung together, and Mexicans, either from Northern California or Southern California, hung together. Inmates usually stayed in their groups, with the exception of some congregating. Problems due to interracial fights are seen as riots, but intra-racial conflicts were just seen as conflicts. Lockdowns would usually happen after a riot. During a lockdown the shot callers involved in the conflict are interviewed together with the C.O.'s. If a particular racial group was not involved then that race can sometimes have access to the yard while the races involved in the conflict continue to be in lockdown. Disrespect between one race and another race usually elicited conflict. After awhile both, all, or one shot caller agrees to let go of the anger, this calms things down, and privileges are returned. Any severe violence results in a total lockdown. Our lives always seemed beyond our control.

One Sunday after church, a very devoted and helpful lifer inmate who ran the Christian service was just sitting there watching television when another white guy cut his throat. His murderer was the opposite of him—he was very huge, tall, and covered with a lot of tattoos (even facial ones). We all ran to the other side of the room while guards were yelling, "Man down!" Everyone had to be in a prone position while the guards responded to the buzzer of the building. Red sirens were flashing everywhere in the building. I was saying to myself while in the prone position, as I looked around to make sure no one was attacking me, "We are going to be in lockdown for a long time."

During my first four months at Pleasant Valley, I kept to myself and ran my own program; I did my normal routine, minding my own business, working out, and running. On a very hot Saturday I didn't pay attention to my surroundings, which was unusual for me. Earlier that day I noticed other races were gathering but I wasn't alarmed. I kept working out on the bar and did my own thing. I was not focused on anyone else. Suddenly I was hit upside the head from behind. I was really dazed but gained my consciousness fast. Then I heard the guards shouting, "Man down! Everyone down, down!" Apparently, a riot was going on. The yard was overcrowded with men in green uniforms. Mace and beanbag guns were everywhere. Shots were fired in the air. Some inmates fell down and some kept fighting. Inmates dropped to their bellies when the guards on the towers shot their guns in the air.

I later found out that a Hispanic inmate known as a South Sider hit me. Four South Siders were stomping one black inmate in one area of the yard while a group of blacks were fighting other South Siders. The C.O.'s assumed that I was part of the riot and that I was hit simply because of my color. The yard was not as cool as I thought it to be. There was nothing cool about prison. But I thought this program yard, where people wanted to go home as badly as I did, cared about the consequences of their actions. Sad to say, I guess not. After escorting us to our cells, we were locked down for many months. Lockdowns resulted in controlled chow lines divided by racial orientation. After we got our food we were locked up again. Freedom of movement was gone. No yard, no church, and no visits. Lockdown was major. Even if you were married, you were not allowed conjugal visits. One bad apple had the capacity to spoil privileges for the whole yard.

While prison could be described as hell on earth, I think back and realize that prison did teach me the discipline of learning a trade and the best practices of communication. Assertive communication in a normal manner is better than forceful communication. These practices helped me in prison and in society when I was released.

10

Nevada City – More Charges

I could hear keys jingling at 5:30 a.m. when the C.O. tapped on the door and told me to "roll it up." This meant I needed to roll up all my belongings and put them into a sheet. I was told that I was going to R&R before going to my court appearance. I was so happy and excited that I got down on my knees and said a prayer of thanks to God for answering my appeal out of L.A. County. I soon realized that this wasn't what that was all about. Two men in cowboy hats dressed in green chained me to the inside of the van. Written on their shirts was "Nevada County Sheriff." At first I thought it meant going out of state to Nevada or that this was a mistake. Maybe I was going back to L.A. for a sentence modification regarding the appeal that I had worked on for eight months because of the harsh sentence I received.

I was the only inmate on the bus. This was not the Grey Goose and the sheriffs were actually friendly. I was alone and enjoying the scenery. The sheriffs told me I was being taken to Nevada City so I asked where that was located. One of them replied, "Nevada City is located next to Grass Valley. Have you ever been there? You must have a warrant there." Then I remembered that I had done a check transaction that had finally caught up with me. I wondered why L.A. hadn't found out about the situation up north and included it with the last charges. Little did I realize what I was up against.

I always seemed to appreciate the views as I was transported to the different facilities. Focusing on the beauty outside the bus was always calming and helped to decrease my anxiety. Snow was beginning to fall and it looked beautiful outside as we made our way to the Wayne Brown Correctional Facility in Nevada City.

I changed from my state "blues" into an "orange"-colored jumper and I was booked. They told me I would have my appearance in court the following Monday morning at 8:00 a.m. The sheriffs were very nice and I greatly appreciated that. Things appeared a bit more civilized in Nevada City. I was in a dormitory with carpeting and a microwave although the bars, small windows, and padded doors were still a part of the scene. The court was down the hallway and I could see both the outside and the dayroom. There was a big screen TV on the wall with a remote nearby on the coffee table. This sure was different from the filth I experienced at the L.A. facility. It looked as though people had it good up in the hills. I felt out of place even though I hadn't been around anyone else yet. Then I noticed many of the faces I would see were mostly white. It didn't mean anything to me until the following morning. The controller clicked open the cell locks for the start of our three-hour dayroom stint. I immediately went to the phone to make a call. There were two phones for 30 men and I was the only black man in the room. Most of the inmates had violated parole. The Nazi Riders were in the cell and had lightning-bolt tattoos on their necks and faces. This was a sign of what I could possibly expect from them. I wasn't fearful at that point because I had a natural way of getting along with others. I was aware but uneasy. I had learned from experience to "pay attention." As I picked up the phone the shortest guy in the tank tapped me and said, "Hey nigger, put down the phone!

My homeboy is going to be trying again!" I thought, How ironic, but whatever, homeboy! I wasn't angry or surprised because my education and experience helped me to stay calm and think. They were taunting me and I had a feeling this wasn't going to stop. About a dozen of the men approached me as a pack and tried to jump me. I shouted to the deputy and I was removed to Protective Custody (PC). Normally PC is for snitches and child molesters, but in this case I was placed in there to protect my life, due to the color of my skin.

The madness was still happening so I stayed in my own cell. I had a visit from the public defender assigned to me. He was very different from the attorney I had in L.A. He looked the part of a mountain man complete with long white hair, beard, jeans, and boots. He told me I wasn't going to like what he was about to tell me. He informed me that I was going to be fighting 25 years to life. "What?!!! I just finished fighting 25 years to life and took a deal for 15 years." He said that this charge wasn't running concurrently with the charges in L.A. so I would be fighting it again. I shouted, "Oh my God! You have got to be kidding me!" I held it together by trying to keep the feelings of numbness I felt as a result of the shocking news. When I was in my cell later, the thoughts of what I would be facing frightened me and kept me up all night.

Still, there was something about this small town that made me feel safe even though I was dealing with the prejudice from the inmates. I was in court with my public defender, the bailiff, and the court reporter while we all waited for the judge. It was a small courtroom that reminded me of the Old West. It was quite the contrast from the big, modern, and crowded courtrooms in L.A. A long 40 minutes passed before the judge entered the courtroom. This seemed odd to me.

The judge finally entered the courtroom, took his seat relaxed and happy; I hoped this meant he wouldn't be prejudiced but a fair judge. I hoped he would be on my side and be able to see what I was experiencing with the long sentence I had been given, and my fear of additional time; it was all quite shocking and overwhelming. Just then my public defender told me in a low voice that he had good news. My heart was beating fast and I prayed that the charges were dropped. Unfortunately, this wasn't exactly what happened. I nodded yes when the judge asked if I knew why I was there. He stated I was being charged with two counts of forgery in the amount of $600.00. He said, "We do things differently here in Nevada County. We take things slow. Please excuse us for being so slow in coming out this morning."

The deputy district attorney smiled at me to show his support also. The judge said he was unable to drop the charges but he was going to run them concurrently with my charges in L.A. This meant that the 15 years I was already serving would not be increased. My time would remain at 15 years. Thank God! This was their way of fixing the judgment error in L.A. where I was excessively sentenced. This was a dream come true for me, an answered prayer. This was so different than L.A., in which they rushed through sentencing. Nevada City took the time to analyze my situation and I was thankful for it.

The following day the Grey Goose came to pick me up with the inmates who were prison-bound. As I left Nevada City and watched the beautiful scenery, I wondered if my time would be reclassified at Pleasant Valley by being reduced from 15 years to 11 years. It happened. The committee lowered my points and took me out of Close Custody B. Due to my low points, after my trail in Nevada County I was transferred to Avenal State Prison, which was a Level 2 facility. My sentence was reduced to 11 years, which really meant 9.5 years with good behavior. This was a positive change but it still seemed like a long road to freedom.

Avenal State Prison was similar to Pleasant Valley and was set up like the Pentagon except the housing was dormitory style—it held 350 men in each dorm. Twelve men shared a cubicle the size of a small living room. There were 12 bunks, 12 lockers, and little space for movement. There was a little more freedom in prison terms but there was a lack of privacy. When I say "lack of privacy," I mean that anyone can open your bedroom or bathroom door unexpectedly. Basically no body function is private—not yours or those of anyone else. I was held there for two years and earned a certificate as a welder through the Prison Industry Authority (hereafter P.I.A.). Even though I only earned $19.00 a month, $.45 cents an hour, working a nine-to-five job in a factory felt like a little bit of freedom.

11

Folsom State Prison

When two years were done at Avenal State Prison in 2000, my points were lowered again. They reclassified me and transferred me to Folsom State Prison. My release date of 2005 seemed like a long way off, but I was making progress. I tried to comfort and encourage myself to feel that God was working with me in my situation. When we rolled up into the city of Folsom, I was deceived again. Mesmerized and captivated by a long road lined with gorgeous oak trees overlooking beautiful Folsom Lake temporarily shifted me from the nightmare that awaited me. The beautiful scenery quickly shifted to tall, old, ugly, and dark gray brick walls. The towers were high above our heads. After the gates closed, all the feelings from the past flooded over me again, including all those familiar nightmarish sounds. I saw people I had been incarcerated with before and I came to the realization that I knew the ropes. I was a convict myself, prison smart and all. My whole life had changed. There was a whole world of codes and ethics I had become attuned to.

Folsom Prison was creepy, dark, old, and gray. The entry process was all too familiar, being constantly indoors and stripped down— the same protocol over again. I was assigned to the largest building, which held 7,000 inmates in five tiers. They placed me in a culinary position as a food server with 27 other inmates. I hated that job. Food from the kitchen was hustled and taken back to the buildings for a quick sale. Anything that was easily accessible was a valuable commodity to the inmates. Popular items included powdered and/or boiled eggs, and bags of peanut butter. Eventually the kitchen food could be traded for canteen food, which included canned items such as tuna, sardines, mackerel, kippers, ham, refried beans, chili, rice, chips, Snicker bars, Musketeers, licorice, Pepsi, ice-cream bars, and so forth. The Kool-Aid was referred to as "Jim Jones"—drink it and you die. "Jim Jones" was so concentrated. One hundred packets of it (single servings) sold for two stamps. These weren't regular postage stamps, but a stamp indicating a value of money. These stamps helped you buy more valued foods.

All these "goodies" came from the "canteen," a special store for inmates that had a money system. In order to obtain canteen food, you had to be available when they did the "draw." The draw went by an inmate's prison number. If you missed your once-per-month draw, you had to wait another month in order to get your canteen food. Prison food with no canteen food was depressing. It was all about surviving in a terrible situation. The inmates who were able to spend over $70.00 per month were referred to as "ballers" (dealers). An inmate's once-a-month chance could be missed because of a riot, lockdown, cell search, or even rain. Inmates had a choice of how much they wanted to spend from their accounts on their chance. I spent all of my $65.00 monthly earnings from license plate creation job due to fear of a lockdown with no canteen access. Canteen items were collected in clear plastic bags that the C.O.'s gave out; everything had to be visible. After all of the canteen items were collected, we would rush back to our cells to hide our valuable items since they were like gold to us in there. Those who didn't have canteen privileges would target those who did. Looking back now, I can't believe how valuable I thought these items were to me.

Making license plates was one of the best paying and most desirable jobs. The factory was large and loud. The plates came down a long revolving belt surrounded by inmates on either side doing their assigned tasks. It was hard and fast work that lasted from 6:30 a.m. to 3:30 p.m. There were few breaks. We were strip-searched before returning to our cells. As humiliating as it was, I became used to the routine. I never risked being caught with anything that would cause me to be thrown in the "Hole" (solitary confinement).

My friend Joe, who'd worked with me at the Bel-Air Supermarket prior to my arrest, visited me every other weekend for three years. He took the time to write me letters that preached Christianity and the need to repent for our sins. He was a good friend and helped to keep me centered through the word of God. I felt that I was meant to meet him; his visits were awesome. During visits, I could smell the scent of women's perfumes, see people with their families, and watch children running around. Visits were awkward, though, because the guards were strict; they had power over us. Regardless, the time with friends and family was very important. Unfortunately the rules and regulations were endless. The tables were low to the ground. One's knees were easily seen so that nothing could be passed. The perimeter of the room was taped to create a barrier for the inmates so they couldn't use the vending machines or the microwave for visitors only.

The inmates' hands needed to be in full sight of the guards, and there was to be no intimate touching. About every hour, we were allowed to go outside to a small area to walk around a rectangular-shaped grassy area. One of the inmates would have a Polaroid camera in order to take pictures, which he would turn right around and sell to the visitors. There were so many restrictions like hands had to be show-ing, we couldn't put one arm around another. We could only stand side by side. As good as it was to visit with the outside world, it was a poignant and sad reminder of how different the lives we lived were. When visiting time was over, it was always so hard to return to our cells and face the sad reality of our lives.

Fortunately, working out and doing my routine in the yard helped me keep my sanity and release my pent-up energy. I kept my earphones on and jumped rope with intensity and did my bar work and dips. Exercising helped me to focus on something positive and gave me a sense of maintaining control in my life.

The two hours in this intense daily routine kept me sharp both men-tally and physically. Faith is all about discipline. We hope and strive with our minds, bodies, and souls.

Compared to other prisons, the Folsom yard was terrible in that it was half the size of a football field with a dirt baseball field in the center. There was a dirt track for walking and the rule was no more than three people side by side.

More than three was considered to be rat packing, which was not al-lowed as it might lead to ganging up on another group, which could initiate a riot and lockdown.

Some inmates thought of me as arrogant. I was in many riots but I never had to fight due to my survival tactic of mingling in a positive way, or being by myself when I sensed that it was the best tactic. I have always enjoyed being with people of different races and cul-tures. I have a natural feeling of feeling at ease and finding interest in others.

12

Avenal State Prison

Every two years there is a classification committee date where in-mates are relocated to another facility in order to prevent over-famil-iarity with the C.O.'s, so that things can be kept more objective and professional. Being moved from one prison to another doesn't mean the inmate is dangerous. This is the way the prison system is designed for the best results. In 2003, I was transferred back to Avenal State Prison to complete my sentence, which meant I only had 20 months left to serve. This was a level-two prison—remember the lower the level, the more freedom there is and less security. I was now in a dormitory that had cubicles and large lockers. Each yard had its own reputation; according to the inmates

- Yard One was considered to be the best.

- Yard Two was the gang members' yard.

- Yard Three was the main culinary yard, which did not offer the P.I.A. trades.

- Yard Four provided education.

- Yard Five was the program yard and a good one.

- Yard Six was referred to as "rockin' and rollin'," meant for the inmates that couldn't get with the program. Yard Six also housed the "Hole."

Five months before I was to be paroled, I got into some more trouble!!! I had not resorted to physical violence because I had always been able to talk my way out of altercations. Basketball was my thing in Yard Five, which had the feeling of a boot camp. I was playing one-on-one with a guy from Riverside who I didn't know very well. His hometown made a difference in the rules because he was from Southern California, and I was considered a Northerner. We played pick-up games every now and again. I had no idea who I was dealing with. We got into an argument on the court; this led to a short fat guy walking up to me, jumping in my face, and demanding why I was talking to his homeboy like that. I was on the court walking backwards, biting my tongue to hold back a verbal fight. The code was that if you are disrespected you handle your business. I was a programmer—an inmate who followed the rules of the C.O.'s program rather than the rules of the convicts. I didn't want an altercation due to my impending release in just five months. This scenario created a big problem with the other convicts. As a result of this incident, the other inmates saw me being disrespected and doing nothing about it. Because the inmate didn't touch me, I felt that I didn't have to react in any way. Since I was known as a programmer and a Christian, I was usually respected, but I guess this was different. I guess they wanted me to stick up for myself. But the rules outside are different from the rules in prison. You don't have the freedom to do what you want. You don't have freedom. I was trying to get out of prison as soon as possible. By the time I returned to the dorm, the Sacramento people that liked me saw what took place on the court and said, "What's up, my nigga? What was that all about, you all right?" I responded, "Yeah, I'm cool. I ain't trippin'. I just want to go home." I walked upstairs to my cubicle, sat on my bunk, and reflected how close I came to fighting and messing up my time. I told myself to "keep it together"…"just a little while longer." Then I heard from a gang member. "Man, you run with us and he disrespected you. That reflects on us. That ain't cool!" I didn't want the situation to get out of control but now I was under pressure. Even though all I did was eat with these guys and play an occasional game of dominos, I was considered to be part of them— homies. Since the Southerners disrespected me, the Northerners saw it as a reflection on them because I was one of them. They didn't like that I wasn't going to do anything about it.

As I walked out of my cubicle and made my way back downstairs, I had everyone's full attention. You could feel the tension in the air while everyone waited to see what would happen next. On my way over to where the short and fat Southerner was sitting with his homeboys, one of the shot callers stopped me and asked me what I was doing. He warned me not to go over. I told him I just want to "holla" (talk) at him and was planning on nothing more than that. With the pressure of being watched, knowing the code, and trying to withhold my anger, this guy was now in my face. I had no choice at this point—either beat him up or get beat up badly by others for disrespecting myself. I popped him in the face and we began wail-ing on each other. I came out the winner. The C.O.'s began shouting, "Man down, man down!" All the inmates dropped to the ground. I heard the jangling of keys and we were both sprayed with mace and escorted out. I was taken to the Hole, where I spent the next 30 days. I lost my privileges, which meant no yard time, one meal per day, one sheet, and one pair of boxers, a t-shirt, and a roll of toilet paper. I didn't feel much like a winner. Something good came out of it though. I began praying and speaking to God more. My faith increased greatly as I imagined having the strength to choose positive things in my life and my future.

After doing the 30 days in the Hole, I was reclassified. It was like starting over. My release changed from five months to eight months. I was transferred to Yard One with the snitches, child molesters, gang dropouts and programmers like myself. This was the only option for those who couldn't exist in the other yards. The C.O.'s felt bad for me because they knew I wasn't a troublemaker. But I remembered God's word: "God sometimes allows evil to happen in order for good to come." Looking back, this whole incident turned out in a positive light. I was put into the Phoenix House Substance Abuse Program that was part of Yard One, "the best yard." About a month later, I noticed a bunch of guys coming out of a trailer, holding what looked like class folders. I asked about it and they told me about a program called SAP (Substance Abuse Program). I was able to apply for a position and become a mentor and T.A. (Teaching Assistant). My role was to perform skits, run groups, and be a T.A. I took classes and obtained certifications in treating substance abuse, child abuse, and anger management. I felt this was my calling and could see this as something I could do in the future. Praise God. "For I know the plans I have for you," declares the LORD, "plans to prosper you and not to harm you, plans to give you hope and a future" (Jeremiah 29:11).

Sixty days prior to release inmates sign parole papers and discuss parole plans with a guidance counselor. This is an exciting time as freedom is quickly approaching. I heard my name called from the podium in the dorms. "S-time ducket" means you're going home soon. It serves as a time of transition to get one's head in order. There's no more SAP—just hanging out for the remainder of the time to think ahead and plan for the future outside of prison.

One day my counselor called me in and handed me a packet of parole conditions to sign. I couldn't believe what I was reading. The conditions were harsh and I was being assigned to Placer County, where I knew no one. I had hoped and planned to be paroled to my sister's house in Southern California. Now I feared being homeless. I expressed my worry to my counselor and he said he had no control over it as the orders came from region one up north. I felt that the conditions were unacceptable but I was informed that unless I initialed every one of them, I would be placed in the Hole for noncompliance. I left my guidance counselor's office feeling confused and angry about what just happened. I decided to stop at the SAP building on the way back to my bunk to speak with one of the counselors. They were the only staff that showed consistent empathy and concern about the inmates' future. I was fortunate to speak with a counselor named Marty. She worked with me on the possibilities. Because I had graduated from the SAP program, I was eligible for a live-in program called SASKA (Substance Abuse Service Coordinating Agency). I was going to be placed in a program called "Help, Hope and Healing in Auburn, California." This was my ticket to having a roof over my head and a valid parole address. I was told that I would be picked up by one of the program's van, thankfully not the "Grey Goose."

On the eve of my parole, the Christian group gave me a spread of food and offered advice as many of them had been paroled but violated it. I was sure that I would never be in their shoes and end up back in prison. I had no idea how difficult it was being on parole. The SASKA van came to pick me up early the next morning. I was the only passenger and the drive was cool; they talked with me along the way. We even stopped at Taco Bell, which was like gourmet heaven to me. I got sick because of the amount of food I ate. It just tasted so good. I wasn't used to what everyone else thought of as normal food.

13
Paroled to Placer

Arriving at the office of HOPE, HEALTH and HEALING in Auburn, California, I had feelings of relief but felt shocked at the same time. I was the only black person there. As I was being introduced, I thought, *Wow. I am finally out of prison.* I sat on the leather sofa with all my belongings in a plastic bag. I didn't have much after living out of a locker for so many years. I hated the shame of being locked up like an animal and never wanted to see the backseat of a police car again. I realized I had many shortcomings in my life and it was time to make amends. The joy of life is in giving—not taking. I felt a sense of humility and could see that being self-centered caused many of my problems. I understood that people had been doing good things for me and that I was so ungrateful. I realized I carried a sense of entitlement. When I entered prison, I was filled with self-pity, anger, and resentment. Through my religious beliefs in finding God and choosing Christ, I was able to realize my strengths and begin to make the positive changes that were necessary in order to be whole, in order to be who I was purposed to be. I know in my heart that sometimes despite our shortcomings, "Life is not easy."

To this day, though, I still believe that I was given an unfair and excessive sentence in light of the fact that my crimes weren't violent.

I was in the Auburn program for three months with others who had served time and were starting over. It looked as though I was the only one who was never a drug user. This did not play out well with the others, as we were still used to the prison code and the fact that I wasn't a user was an issue for them. None of us were very familiar with all the new technology from the last decade, and this affected our adjustment as well.

After three months there, I was told to walk (to leave). This was the best thing for me because of all the negativity I was getting from the four guys I lived with (mostly because I was not a drug user). However, I was happy that I left with a valid driver's license because it was very necessary for employment. My friend Joe who visited me in prison was associated with a church. Both he and the church continued their support for me. After being asked to leave the program, I had no place to stay. I called Joe from a pay phone one day (as I was not allowed to have a cell phone). He prayed for me and took me to see my parole officer. I moved in with one of the members from the church I attended in Sacramento.

After the housing issue was settled I began to work for this guy named Todd cleaning and detailing cars at a dealership next to the parole office near Grass Valley. Through Todd's help, I was able to get a car, which led to delivering car parts to the towns around Grass Valley. Eventually, I became a car salesman in Auburn. After making $64.00 per month in prison, I was thrilled to be making $5,000.00 a month doing honest work. I was so happy to be wearing a suit and tie instead of an orange jumpsuit! I trusted Todd—he was the only person who knew I was on parole. My first parole officer was a man named Roy.

He called me into his office to ask me how I had obtained a sales license. After I gave him the information, he turned to another officer and said, "See, I told you!" Roy was nice to me but I wasn't aware that some of the other officers made fun of the parolees. A week later he asked me if I would like to speak with the inmates who were going to be released from prison soon. This was a great opportunity, and I felt complimented because of what I had achieved after being out for a mere 11 months.

I began to relax and was so happy that things were going well working in Auburn. I stuck to my parole restrictions and I kept that part of my life a secret. It was too easy to get a complaint, which could turn into a violation especially if anyone wanted to take advantage of my situation. One day the other salesmen and myself were told that we were being transferred to the Roseville Ford dealer-

ship. This made me extremely happy because I would be only 10 minutes away from my condo. The next day we all packed our items and customer information files from our desks at work to take care of until the other job started. When I returned to my condo, I placed everything on my desk at home to take to work with me when my new job began in the following week. The files contained basic information on various customers, such as driver licenses and credit histories. I had seen the files so many times and so I paid no attention to the material while waiting to take it to the dealership. I was very happy with my condo and the people I had met in the eight months that I lived there. I paid my rent on time and didn't cause any problems.

I felt confident about myself, my job, and about my interaction in society. I loved wearing a suit and tie every day. It was a great feeling to be functioning so well.

When my parole officer (P.O.) made his first visit, he was surprised to see how nice my home and car was. A parolee has to keep the P.O. informed of his residence, car, and so on or it could be a violation. He told me that I had a very nice place, which was better than most of his parolees, and he seemed satisfied. My mother's decorating abilities had exposed me to a good sense of design, which, I have to admit, is better than most. I asked my P.O. for a 6-day pass on December 11th to visit my family in L.A., and I was given 4 days with the return date being after Christmas. I agreed with this and was so happy at the thought of being with my family, who I hadn't seen in 10 years. It was arranged and I would pick up my pass on December 19th. After he left, I called my sister and we shared our happiness in anticipation of a wonderful reunion. I went shopping for Christmas gifts and kept them in a huge bag in my living room.

About 6:30 p.m. the night before I was going to be driving to L.A., I heard a loud knock followed by "Sanders! Open the door! Now! Police Parole search! Open now!!!" My heart seemed to beat as loud as the knocking. They rushed in, cuffed me, and set me on the couch. The eight cops searched my place with a K-9 unit, looking at everything I owned including the information on my computer. They searched my car and asked how I could afford such nice things.

I was earning good money at my job, which was information they already had. Then one of them took the folder from the desk that had the customer information. I was informed that I would be going to prison if the dealer wasn't aware I had these. They took me to the county jail and I couldn't control the tears. I could not believe that I was going to have everything I worked so hard for be taken away from me. This involved no crime but just my carelessness about keeping the files safe in my house. I was right back in court with a parole violation and fighting a new case with four charges of forgery, stolen property, and identity theft. I couldn't believe this and was angry at what was happening. The charges meant that CDC could violate me because of the contact with the cops. This was now an additional case with 60 days in the county jail. I was still fighting my case in Placer County Superior Court.

The Roseville County Jail was cold and dark and I was in tears. What in the hell was going on?! I was scared and mad at the same time. The biblical passage Romans 8:37, "...We are more than conquerors and gain a surpassing victory through Him who loved us...," came to mind. My automatic response for any kind of sorrow and stress is to turn to God for comfort, and this passage had special meaning for me under the circumstances. I was snatched out of my new world with a job, car, apartment, and friends and thrown back into what I thought had been resolved at the last court hearing and the price I'd paid. This time, I had done nothing to have put me into this place. In the back of my mind, I feared that something would happen because I was doing so well and had been through so much to have at last gotten to a positive place in my life. None of the charges were true.

The next day, I was bussed to the Auburn County Jail where all the inmates there are fighting charges or have been arrested, and are to be held until the parole officer or court could make a determination. I knew that I would be charged with a violation. I had no idea what was going on until the next day when I went down the hall chained to another detainee in orange. We all sat on a long bench waiting to see a free public defender. Those who can pay were able to see a private attorney. I knew that no matter what I was going to do, I was going to have a private attorney. My life is not a game of chance, and my only hope was to have the best possible defense attorney caring for my case. The public defender approached me, leaned over, and gave his name. He said that I was fighting 25 to life. I said, "No, I'm not." I asked the judge for a week's delay in order to hire a private attorney, which was granted. "So may it be, Mr. Sanders, you have a week...and do you understand the seriousness of these charges?" I responded, "Yes, I do, Your Honor, and thank you." I felt strongly that I made the decision with the best possible result based upon past experience and listening to the experiences of others with whom I'd discussed this within jail. I felt it too strongly in my gut to go against my feeling. I realize there are exceptions, but I was unwilling to take the chance with my life for a third time—especially since this time it could affect me for the rest of my life. It was unbelievable that, once again, I was fighting 25 to life!!! When they say three strikes you're out, they really mean it. The county jails in Placer County were in huge tanks and so much better than the L.A. and other jails in which I had served time. There was a dayroom with about 35 guys in the "pod" and amenities such as television, hot plates for both lunch and dinner, weekly visits, and no segregation. I began to contact friends, and a woman that I was seeing loaned me $4,000.00 for an attorney. She set me up with Woodall and Leupp, a law firm in Auburn with an excellent reputation. I was told they were the best out of all the others. Timothy Woodall spoke with me at length. He realized that I felt it would kill me if I were sent back to prison. I spent four months in the county jail, which was the same amount of time I received for my violation delays while my case was being processed. During that time, my mother had a stroke and passed, and my oldest brother Lamont died from kidney disease.

Things were really bad and all I could do was trust in God. I thanked him for letting me stay in the county jail rather than prison during this time. I started reading *The Word*, which is a Christian daily reading of scripture, stories, and excerpts from the sermons. This was something I knew how to do from my days as a convict, which kept me feeling positive and helped me to stay sane no matter what came my way.

"God has given us knowledge, power and a sound mind" (2 Timothy 1:7). This had become a familiar way of functioning in tough times, and it really worked for me. Any mental, physical, or emotional pain is increased tremendously when you are behind bars. Over the years, I learned that trust in God was my saving grace whenever I felt abandoned, betrayed, or rejected. For people on the outside who forget about you or don't care, life goes on. I learned this through my experience that I can have "victory over" the pain, instead of being a "victim of" the pain. You can too!

I knew the truth would come out in court with the help of my new attorneys. I was fighting for my freedom so I wouldn't spend the rest of my life in prison for crimes I didn't commit. These trumped-up charges could have the effect of putting me away forever. At the court hearing, I was charged with identity theft because I had information from potential customers that could have been used in a criminal way. The files I had taken home from the Dodge dealership while waiting for the Ford dealership job to begin were necessary for business purposes. Other salespeople would also keep files at home for various reasons. I had been asked to clear my desk, which involved taking care of the files and keeping them safe.

I believe the P.O. who did the parole search was surprised when he saw that I had purchased nice things like my car, furniture, and clothes. My income of $5,000 to $6,000 a month afforded me the option of buying nice things. I was used to having a well-designed home and nice clothes, as these are things I grew up with. I believe he didn't think I legitimately bought these things with my hard-earned money. So that's why they did a parole/police sweep when those eight officers came to my door. They were looking for something to explain it all. As a result, I was now facing my Third Strike.

Timothy Woodall responded to each one of the charges and at the last minute declared that he had two witnesses. The D.A. was unaware that my former Dodge boss and the Ford boss were there to testify. This was an excellent strategy by my attorney. After their testimony, which confirmed that I was keeping the files in my apartment until my Ford dealership position began, all the charges were dropped. Only God! The D.A. was completely caught off guard and surprised. I know he wasn't happy with the outcome. Since I went four months without a paycheck, I lost all that I had worked so hard for—my apartment, car, and credit-card payments were all behind. I was advised by parole that I couldn't work at the dealership anymore because they wanted to keep me out of trouble. I knew the explanation was bogus. People were prejudiced and trying to keep me down. *Yeah...this would keep me out of trouble—when I never really was in trouble to begin with.* I had to deal with this loss and go on. I found a house in Roseville that rented rooms and it was a nice place to stay. My friend of 13 years, Mr. Scott, offered me a job in Sacramento working with teens that were having a difficult time coping and staying in school. I was not allowed to move to Sacramento because I had no family there. I was allowed to move to L.A. but because of the two deaths in my family, I didn't want to go back there. I wanted a fresh start.

Three months later I was hit with a new charge of perjury. I was being accused of lying on my sales license application. I had been honest and told my boss that I was on parole when I was hired. The same D.A. who had lost the last case against me and was trying to make those three strikes become a reality initiated this new charge. You know it seems like you are never really free, but with Christ in every circumstance we are free indeed. Court was different this time. I was out of my custody and parole and knew I was fighting for my life. They thought there was a possibility that I might run. I let them know that I wanted to prove my innocence and to be set truly free indeed.

Running was not something I would consider doing. I kept my same attorneys and the same judge I had before I was assigned to the case. We were outside in the hallway of the courthouse when my attorney turned to me and said, "You won't like this, but I advise you to take the four years he is giving you and you will be out in two and still be young enough to start over." I said, "What?! This is nuts. I am not guilty!" I let my friends talk with them and I went outside. I stood between two cars and prayed through the tears thinking of my options. I walked into the courtroom ready to face the judge with my attorney. I spoke up and fired him. The judge said, "Mr. Sanders, do you know what you are doing? You are fighting the low end of a life sentence." If I lost, I would be in jail for the rest of my life. I said, "I'm not guilty and I would like new counsel in this matter." The judge said, "Okay, I will give you a month." This gave me time because I was put on the spot to take four years or life in prison. There was no reasonable deal; I wasn't guilty. I strongly felt God's influence about this decision.

Two weeks later at a bar and grill, I met Mike Wise, an attorney. The name even sounded like God chose him. He agreed to take my case. Mike is a former D.A. from Sacramento County. His experience of being a prosecutor and a defense attorney give him a unique understanding of the system. He was my best chance at attaining justice. If we lost the case, I would potentially spend the rest of my life in jail. I couldn't have been more fearful knowing this but I wasn't going to run. I'd finally learned my lesson and had done nothing wrong. Jesus told his disciples to understand how much discipline it took to maintain faith. Mike and I went to court several times over this charge, and it took months to negotiate with the D.A. on the matter. We could not get an agreement of any kind of deal to put on the table so we set a date for trial. I had difficulty sleeping, as I was full of anger at the possibility of spending the rest of my life in prison.

I was in shock and depressed as to what my life had become. There were so many conditions of parole that I was unable to go almost anywhere without prior approval, or it could be a violation. I thought I would lose everything. What else was scary was that I would likely be facing an all-white jury in Colfax. I feared that facing Three Strikes, especially as a black man, could have a major influence on the outcome. The only thing that was right was that I had Mike Wise to represent me. "The truth shall set you free." For me, my truth and my hope were having Mike as my attorney.

During those months, I saw an educational psychologist. He tested and evaluated me for a learning disability that impacts reading and writing and in my case, filling out forms. This brought back memories of being in a special education class dealing with my dyslexia. This made sense to me that the results of the test were a crucial part of the defense in my case, and my success. Isn't God good! Now I'm writing a book. Don't let the devil take your hope. The devil is trying to steal, kill, and destroy. Don't let the devil take nothing from you. Pray, pray, and pray some more. A good prayer to pray is, "Help me, Lord!" I reported in to parole consistently and was being watched carefully. Home searches continued and I wasn't sure if they really thought I was doing something wrong or if they just wanted to get me back in custody.

The day arrived when I received a call from my attorney, Mike, that the verdict was in and that I needed to meet him at the Roseville Courthouse instead of in Colfax. The jury had spent two weeks considering all of the evidence regarding my filling out the application, and in terms of testing, how I perceived the information I was asked to provide. The expert who tested me and the other independent teacher (both in the same field) testified at my trial.

Sitting in the courtroom, I could almost hear my heart beating. The 12 jurors filed into the jury box. Some were tearful and one winked at me. I turned to Mike, who acknowledged with a facial expression that he had seen the same thing, which appeared, hopefully, to be a positive sign. We all stood up to listen to the verdict. The guards moved behind me on either side. Are they getting ready to handcuff me? I was filled with fear and anxiety. Mike held my hand. It meant so much to me to feel his support physically like a great friend or father. The lesser charge of False Statements (Vehicle Code section 20) was heard first and the result was "Not Guilty." Then came the higher charge of Perjury by Declaration or Certification (Penal Code section 118), which was a felony that could put me away forever. The bailiff read the verdict for that charge and I jumped for joy. "Not Guilty." I was so happy that I couldn't even let down my tears until I returned home, where I cried for a long time. It was very hard on my soul to have faced that day.

After the verdict was read, I turned to the D.A. and said, "Thank you for the test. I have learned to take my time and pay attention when I fill out an application for anything." He didn't seem to like the way that I spoke to him and that I was free of the charges. Some of the jury stayed around and asked me questions. Some wished me luck and others said a few good words. For me, this day was a huge victory/success. I kept hugging Mike. I felt it was God's work of granting me the privilege of having my life continue, while being able to tell my story to others who are facing the impact of the Three Strikes Law. I pray my story will give hope to those who are not guilty or to those suffering so long for an unreasonable confinement.

WISE LAW GROUP

428 J Street #200 | Sacramento, CA | O: 916.467.9473 | F:916.476.4023

It has been my pleasure to know Ralph Sanders for several years. He is my client and my friend.

I met Ralph in my office, when he contacted me about a legal matter on which he needed representation. My initial impression of Ralph as he laid out the details of his personal history and then current legal challenges was that there must be some mistake; In front of me sat a man professionally dressed, genuine in his demeanor and eagerly committed to excelling in life. As Ralph explained his circumstances, I was immediately impressed with his drive to move past his prior mistakes, improve himself as a man and succeed on levels that he did not then completely understand.

Since that initial meeting, I have watched, encouraged and sat astonished at Ralph's ability to consistently move forward in life armed with charisma, an astonishingly handsome appearance and certain genuineness in his personality capable of defusing the most cynical and hardened individual. Through the course of years I have known Ralph Sanders he has worked tirelessly to improve his station in life, improve himself as a man and to distance himself from the mistakes of his youth. He has succeeded in those efforts, though I've no doubt he intends to continue his path toward personal success and fulfillment.

Our current criminal justice system can stamp a man, break a man and impose great limitations upon his ability to get ahead in life, once he has been convicted of a felony. In my several years of experience in criminal law, Ralph stands out as a man who refused to be labeled, limited or held back by circumstances or even the negative and limiting perceptions of others. He has blossomed into a role model for young men who struggle early in life, but later decide they wish to break the mold society often places them into as a result of youthful indiscretions.

Ralph's experiences provide valuable lessons for men who may feel limited by their past. His trials and struggles are solid proof that the path back to redemption is not easy. However, his will to endure and his strength to succeed also demonstrate the courage necessary to shake the dead skin of past transgressions and move forward in life. Finally, Ralph's continued success is a benchmark for anyone who feels they cannot get ahead in life. Ralph has succeeded and so can you.

Michael J. Wise, Esq.
Sacramento, CA
February, 2011

www.wisechoicelaw.com

Page 1 of 1

Conclusion

I am so thankful for the incredible people that were behind me and gave me advice both in my faith as well as direction for my future. I know that God helped me to use my experiences to shape who I am today, and I am forever thankful and grateful. It is also a true joy to know that I made it through the tough cracks of pressure and time alone facing the unknown. Initially, I never thought these tests could build up my character in a positive way. Dealing with the suffering from the loss of freedom and the pain of abandonment strongly indicates to me again that the Lord uses our experiences as a way to improve us. It's like a fiery test that is not to destroy but to refine. Jeremiah 29:11: "For I know the plans I have for you, declares the Lord, plans to prosper you, and not to harm you, plans to give you hope and a future."

We all know "The future is yours if you want it to be!" I was told this by my high-school basketball coach as an expression of hope that was passed on to graduating seniors. We all know that while some of us grab hold of life with enthusiasm and do as much as we can to take control of our future, such a promise doesn't always pan out for everyone. Why is this? What makes the difference? I know through my trials and suffering that happy, successful, fulfilled individuals are those who learn to live their best in the present time known as NOW.

A person like myself, especially dealing with a mark of Two Strikes, can find comfort by making the best of the present moment. One more Strike and you are out (or, rather, in). Are we able to enhance our future? It is my belief based upon perceptions of my past experience that you can succeed to some great extent with the challenges you are facing though it might seem difficult and hard. You can enjoy your life or even parts of it right now. I have seen many people go through life with low self-esteem. These individuals focus on the negative, feeling inferior or inadequate while dwelling on some reason why they can't have a good life like others around them. We need to focus upon our own lives and our own journey in order to see our full potential. Unfortunately, some never see the other side of true freedom from inside jails, prisons, hospitals, relationships, and the Three Strikes Law!

Since being released from prison, I have been living a lawful life. I got married approximately two years ago and have a beautiful wife and daughter. We are living in the outskirts of Sacramento in a lovely suburban neighborhood.

My daughter is my inspiration. She gives me hope and motivates me every day I see her beautiful smile to become a better person. I am very blessed. I am working with troubled youth that are having problems in society. The program is called Juveniles At Risk (JAR). This job is very rewarding for me as I am able to help teens turn their lives around. I locate potential employers and schedule interviews for these youths to get jobs. I also meet with their probation officers and give them status updates on their behavior and programs they participate in such as the G.E.D. and/or the A.A. I also enjoy coaching young teens in basketball and being a mentor to help them stay on track in life.

Another passion of mine is to speak at programs such as halfway houses and county jails. In the future, I plan to speak to inmates incarcerated in California's prisons. I get tremendous joy from telling my story and giving hope to others who may feel completely hopeless about their situation. My prayer is that they will hear my story and believe they can turn their lives around.

CPSIA information can be obtained at www.ICGtesting.com
Printed in the USA
BVOW071805051212

307184BV00001B/2/P